A PORTRAIT OF COLORADO

For Lois and Marilyn

A PORTRAIT OF COLORADO

A PORTRAIT OF COLORADO

Text by Thomas K. Worcester and Robert B. Pamplin, Jr.
Paintings and drawings by Susan E. Underwood
Photographs by Thomas K. Worcester

In memory of Doris Y. More
august 1976

By Carl & Virginia Johnson

An OMSI PRESS publication
OREGON MUSEUM OF SCIENCE AND INDUSTRY
Portland, Oregon

Distributed by
The Touchstone Press
P. O. Box 81, Beaverton, Oregon 97005

A PORTRAIT OF COLORADO

I.S.B.N. No. 0-911518-43-6

Library of Congress Catalog Card No. 76-23610

Copyright© 1976 by OMSI PRESS

Oregon Museum of Science and Industry

Design by Robert Reynolds

Printed in the United States of America by
Graphic Arts Center, Portland, Oregon

INTRODUCTION

Millions of words have been written about Colorado. All the proper adjectives have been used—splendid, magnificent, breathtaking, majestic, beautiful, ad infinitum—and all are applicable.

But, even though Colorado has an abundance of natural elegance, the essence of the state's history is in her people: their personalities, their deeds and their creations. So the authors have chosen to show that essence in a variety of media, which, when blended with the display of her natural beauty, attempts to capture the full scope of Colorado's charm. Thus the combination of original art, photographs and written text.

Since art is the substance that can provide romantic glimpses through the rendition of a worn buckboard, a rusted dairy can, or a clapboard blacksmith's shop, paintings and drawings were chosen to reveal part of Colorado's past. Yet these rustic items are very much a part of the scene today, there to be enjoyed by the observant traveller as well as the artist.

For a contemporary Colorado the authors selected the camera, as photography is a medium that can capture the beauty of the state while not attempting to hide the scars of her character.

The final dimension has been added to the visual presentation through the written vignettes that fuse the lore and humanity of Colorado's people with nature's wonders.

This, then, is A PORTRAIT OF COLORADO, a distinct portrayal of the Centennial state.

THE SLEEPING UTE

Once upon a time, there lived in the land of red rock and sage, a band of Ute Indians who had discovered the secret of extended life, and grew to be immense giants, much bigger than the mere mortals of today.

One time the tribe headed north from their homeland, seeking game for the long winter ahead and hides to cover their huge bodies. One Indian brave, strong and courageous, stayed behind to stand guard over their homeland. Though his tribe did not return for days, then weeks and months, he remained in his appointed place, never wandering from the land of the Utes. More months passed, then years, and even decades, and still the tribe did not return. But the young man remained faithful to his duty, standing tall and proud, towering over the buttes and arroyos of the land.

The loyal guardian did not know what fate had befallen his tribesmen. During the time they were in the northland, members of the band had disregarded their ancient Ute customs. In adopting habits that were contrary to their Ute teachings and beliefs, they ignored the Great Spirit.

Great Spirit was angry with the tribesmen. For a long time he pondered the punishment for the giants, and finally he decided to take away the things they cherished most: long life and their huge stature. So, Great Spirit reduced the size of the Ute tribesmen to that of normal human beings, and shortened their life span to that of other mortals.

Meanwhile, the young giant, loyal to the ancient Ute beliefs and true to his promise to his people, had tired and weakened from his long vigil. Finally he was forced to lie down to rest. And when he did, Great Spirit looked upon him with much favor, admiring his strength and his loyalty, Then, Great Spirit said:

"He shall remain on earth, forever asleep, as a memorial to all all that is good in the Ute teachings."

And with that, Great Spirit turned the remaining Ute giant to stone, lying where he was in what now is Montezuma County, Colorado. When his people returned, centuries later, they found the young brave, arms folded across his chest, knees slightly flexed, head turned to the side. And today, visitors to Mesa Verde National Park also can see the Sleeping Ute near the entrance to the park, transfixed in his eternal repose.

TEN-FOOT McGARRITY

No man sought less to be a legend—nor earned it more—than the miner who became known as Ten-Foot McGarrity.

McGarrity, whose given name has long since been lost to the muses of fate, followed the lure of gold to Central City in the 1850's, and was among the hundreds of bearded, red-shirted men who thronged to Russell and Gregory Gulches to help start the Little Kingdom of Gilpin, then thought to be the richest square mile on earth.

McGarrity had no special characteristics that made him stand out from the other miners. He was an ordinary sort—hard working and hard drinking. Occasionally he made a modest strike, and several times he stashed away enough gold to lease a small bit of property, which he worked himself.

But, as the story is told, McGarrity came to the point in his mining career where he was going to make one more all-out challenge of the fickle ore that had alluded him in quantity. This was to be the strike that would make him wealthy, and he put his last dollar into a lease not far from the Gregory diggings. McGarrity swung his pick in earnest, maintaining his energy from a small cache of hard tack and ham. Finally, a "streak" developed under his pick, and McGarrity drove a tunnel, all the time dreaming of how he would spend the yellow wonder that fired his conscience. He made enough from the digging to pay his expenses, but the streak would pay out, then reappear, enticing him like a fickle lover. But nowhere could he find the pocket of gold that would bring him unending wealth.

Finally, McGarrity's dream began to fade. When he had only enough money to stretch through one more week, McGarrity decided to accept the offer of two brothers who wanted to buy his lease.

So, the reluctant—but hungry—McGarrity sold. And when the brothers had driven but ten feet farther into the rock, they struck the pocket of gold the spunky Scot had sought. It was then that McGarrity made a vow:

"I'll never give up a lease again until I've dug just 10 feet farther."

And, according to the old-timers who were his friends, the miner was true to his word, giving rise to the appellation of Ten-Foot McGarrity, by which he then was known.

THE WORTH OF A YELLOW DOG

Harry Clemens was in Prescott, Arizona when he was approached by an elderly gentleman who seemed to recognize him:

"I beg your pardon, Sir, but I believe we have met somewhere."

Clemens looked closely at the venerable accoster, and said:

"Yes, that is quite possible . . . you do look familiar. But, I am not from this area. I am here from Colorado. My name is Clemens, Harry Clemens."

"Ah, ha—Harry Clemens, from Colorado. Yes, that would be it. I lived there for some time, before moving to Arizona. Do you know Judge Steck—Amos Steck?" the stranger inquired.

"Oh, very well," said Clemens. "Indeed, I know the judge quite well."

"Will you give him my respects, then," said the old man. "Steck was my bosom friend. And, did you know George Chilcott?"

"I certainly do," replied Clemens, now a bit puzzled as to the identity of the man.

"Please tell George I harbor no ill feelings for him, if you see him. You see, George and I once sparked for the same woman."

At that, the old man wiped his face with his sleeve, and remarked:

"These old remembrances always bring tears. I just guess I am too sentimental."

"Well, my friend, whom shall I say remembered Judge Steck and Chilcott so fondly?" asked Harry Clemens.

"Howard—John Howard, the attorney, although they call me Judge down here."

"They will, of course, remember you Mr. Howard?"

"Oh, yes, of that I am certain. We all have much to remember. Just mention my name, and I am sure they will remember the old associations. Yes, I am quite sure they will."

"Then consider it done, Mr. Howard. I shall make a special point to see Judge Steck when I return to Denver."

In due time, Harry Clemens returned to Colorado, and as he said he would do, stopped in to see Amos Steck to bring him tidings of John Howard.

"Shucks," said the judge. "Did you meet that fellow? He's a sharpie, that man is. He's the man who sold his wife back in the early days for $75 and a yellow dog. I believe it was a hound. Now, a good woman was hard to come by in those days . . . but I guess a good dog was, too, now that I think about it."

"But how did he sell his wife?" Clemens asked.

"Well, sir, here's the way it was. His wife left him and went with another man. She persisted in living with that other man, in spite of the fact she was married to John. Now, John could have gone after that other fellow with a gun and settled the whole thing that way, and I suspect a jury might have acquitted him. But he saw things another way, and just settled it in a business-like manner. Being a miner, he just quit-claimed the woman for the due consideration I mentioned—$75 and a hound dog. I had a copy of the deed around here somewhere. Ah—here it is.

" 'Territory of Colorado, County of Arapahoe.

" 'This indenture made the second of May, the year of our Lord 1862. Witnesseth that for and in consideration of the sum of $75 of lawful money of the United States and the further valuation of one yellow dog, to be in hand paid by John Doe, I hereby sell, devise, convey and quit claim unto the said John Doe all my rights, title and interest to and in my wife, Rebecca Howard, nee Hightower, together with all and single the improvements and hereditaments therein to the said John Doe and every right I had or may have in said premises. Witness my hand and seal this day of May, 1862. Signed John Howard'

"Yes, sir, a good dog was hard to come by."

THE SPOTSWOOD OXPRESS

Their names were Gus and Charlie, Spank and Bow, Buffo and Babe, Dan and Dandy, and usually they came in pairs. With yokes around their massive necks, they plodded the hundreds of miles from Missouri and Iowa, through Kansas and Nebraska, down the South Platte to Colorado, helping establish a new life for those who directed them.

They were the oxen, the magnificent, big-eyed, patient, faithful, strong animals who pulled the early evidence of civilization across the plains to the Rockies, and on to Oregon and California.

Bullwhackers were a breed of their own. One driver once said:

"There was three things more important to a bullwhacker than anything else. First, he had to know how to use the reins, and know a 'gee' from a 'haw'! Then he had to be able to use a whip. A good whip man could slice a wing off'n a fly from 20 feet away. And, the third thing he had to know was how to cuss. He had to have a fittin' vocabulary of cuss words so's that the oxen could understand him."

In 1873, Col. Bob Spotswood, Colorado's premier stage and express line operator, began using oxen on some of his lines after an epidemic of what was called "epizootic" felled so many horses and mules that none was available for the wagons. Those animals that had not been infected soon were picked up by Wells Fargo and Overland, the big users of good horseflesh. Spotswood had a contract to carry mail from Denver to South Park, via Morrison and Turkey Creek Canyon, but he was unable to find a single horse or mule to use even in an emergency.

Needing to protect his reputation for prompt and efficient service, Spotswood finally located some well-trained oxen that could be substituted for horses, slow as they were. His line was quickly dubbed the "Spotswood Oxpress," which he accepted with good-natured pride.

But on one trip, when Spotswood had an unusually heavy load of mail and express, plus a single passenger, the oxen suddenly stampeded while going through a stand of timber above Slaght's Station. Both Col. Bob and the passenger finally jumped when the animals could not be halted, then watched with dismay as the wagon was demolished and its contents scattered in the snow.

This was the one time in his career when Bob Spotswood left mail and express unguarded. He and his passenger walked several miles upgrade to the station at Kenosha Hill, where they were able to borrow a wagon and get volunteers to help them round up the oxen and the cargo.

But Spotswood's experience with the oxen was a rare occurrence, for generally the bulky animals could be counted on for their even temperament and willingness to perform as desired. Indeed, an admirer of the ox once said:

"Why, the west would never 'f been settled without the ox. Bison still would own the plains, and the white man would be grubbing corn on the other side of the Platte. Colorado still would be run by jack-rabbits, grizzlies, and Indians—and most of us wouldn't even know what we'd missed."

WINTER ON THE PLAINS

The small towns of eastern Colorado are quiet places, with well-kept houses, and a skyline dominated by a grain elevator and a water tower. Trees in the towns often display power-company pruning, and on a frigid December morning, most of the pick-ups parked in front of the cafes have "farm" plates. Inside, the coffee pot replaces the pot-bellied stove or cracker barrel of the past.

A tanned, alert, compact man in a visored cap and heavy overalls talks about the weather:

"Last year we had a foot of snow all winter. This year there hasn't been any real moisture since June, other than a few sprinkles. The winter wheat is up, but that's about all."

Winter on the Colorado plains can be unforgiving. Yet the stock men are ready. High stacks of baled hay are nearby and the corn cribs are full.

Corn once played a more unusual role near Sterling. Valley Station, built in 1859 as a stagecoach stop on the Leavenworth-Pikes Peak express, also was a station for the Overland Trail to California in the 1860's. It was an outpost during the Indian wars of 1864-65, and once was defended by a breastwork of sacks of shelled corn which had been quickly put in place before an impending attack.

Today, the Colorado farmer has to fight the same elements as did his ancestors, but at least he can use his corn for feed.

PASSING OF THE HORSE

It was but a few years back that a horse and buggy squired the family to church, picnic socials, and visits to town for gossip and staples. On many occasions, pride of a horse and a little showmanship would bring a friendly race as carriages passed while on a Sunday afternoon ride. Even parlor talk among men would eventually turn to horses, and who could boast of owning the fastest steed.

Even after the coming of the automobile, the cry "get a horse" became popular.

But a different way of life has come with the "horseless" carriages. Rutted dirt roads have been smoothed and paved, service areas provide the necessary ingredients for insuring a continuous transit, and the cushion of an air-smooth ride has greatly improved dispositions of travelers. The social changes have been more subtle. The pace of life keeps time with the speed of all those "horses under the hood," so that communion with nature requires planning, where before she surrounded each moment, each activity.

Yet the horse still commands respect on the western ranch and is as useful for some chores as it ever was. And maybe if a cowhand's gentle words to his horse could be overheard they might be something like this:

"Don't worry Blue, I ain't turning you in on one of those gas guzzlin' rattletraps, though you ever try to wipe me off on a gate post again and I might think about it. Sure, you eat a lot, but I gotta admit—you'll go even if'n you're empty, and that thing won't budge. I reckon what's most important, though—I can talk to you, an' nobody says I've taken leave of my senses. Least ways they don't say nothin' to me! Can't do that with no Jeep!"

THE LAST BUFFALO?

Springfield was a new frontier town when Patrick Byrnes arrived there a cold, gray day in early February, 1888.

The stage ride from Lamar, 50 miles due north, had been tiresome, though Byrnes was intrigued by the new and strange country through which the coach had rolled. Now he welcomed the heat of the small stove in the hotel lobby in Springfield.

Amid stories of cooking with buffalo chips on sheet-iron stoves or open fires, a man casually mentioned that the last specimen of all the vast and ill-fated herds of buffalo, or American bison, had been shot and killed not far from Springfield a short time before.

Byrnes thought little of the incident until later, while exploring the quarter section of land two miles east of Springfield he had won in the government homestead lottery. At the south end of his land, extending almost across the tract, was the deep, narrow gorge of a canyon that terminated sharply against a solid wall of rock rising in abrupt steps to the level of the surrounding plains. In the canyon was a spring, a familiar watering place for the old scouts and settlers, and known to both wild and domestic animals.

Believing the canyon to be the one he had heard described concerning the last buffalo, Byrnes began at its lower end and followed a cattle trail through scrub brush, greasewood and wild roses, now and then twisting around large boulders that had fallen from the cliffs above. Byrnes was so engrossed in watching a road-runner that had crossed his path, that he nearly overlooked the skeleton of a buffalo laying well under an overhanging ledge, partially hidden by a clump of sage brush.

Curious now about the story, Byrnes made inquiries, and learned that the buffalo had been a young cow that had been seen occasionally in the area for several months before it was shot. It had browsed along the canyon bottom with a small herd of range cattle, and came to be considered a pet by the settlers and townspeople, and regarded even as a rare zoological curiosity. It was shot by a vagabond adventurer, who quickly skipped town when he met the wrath of area residents who considered his deed unpardonable.

Byrnes reached this conclusion:

"As no other wild buffalo had ever been seen in that part of the country, it is reasonable to believe that it was, in truth, the last living specimen of all the vast multitudes of buffaloes that roamed at their free will over that broad expanse of territory lying east of the Rocky Mountains and extending south from the Arkansas River into No-Man's Land."

GEORGE PULLMAN, CLAIM STOMPER

An appointment with sleeper car manufacturer George M. Pullman was harder to get than a visit with the president of the United States in the late 1800's. One visitor to Pullman's Chicago office was met by an officious secretary, who said:

"May I tell Mr. Pullman the nature of your business, General Hall?"

"Well, Ma'm, I recon' you can, but I suspect I'd get to see him faster if you tell him it's Frank Hall, a fellow claim stomper."

The secretary disappeared behind a massive door. Moments later a voice boomed out:

"Frank, is that really you? Come in, man . . . come in."

Such was the new life of George Pullman, self-made millionaire monopolist, who had changed the habits and comforts of American rail travelers. Pullman was not yet 30 when he went to Colorado in 1859. He already had worked on designing a more efficient and comfortable sleeping car and had persuaded the Chicago and Alton Railroad to let him convert three new day coaches. But since the railroads had been reluctant to invest in new equipment, the impatient genius left his business in Chicago and moved on to Colorado, seeking to secure his future in the gold fields near Central City.

George Pullman sold equipment to the miners and at Black Hawk formed a partnership with James Lyon. Pullman and Lyon found it more to their liking to buy gold dust from other miners than to claw through claims, and they turned a profit as brokers. When they started lending money—at up to 50 percent interest—they prospered for a time, although not to the extent that George Pullman had envisioned when he left Illinois.

But when Pullman returned to Chicago in 1863 he took with him something from the boom towns that proved to be more profitable than all the Colorado gold that had passed through his hands—an idea. Pullman had observed the pulldown bunks in the flop houses where the miners slept, and the scheme fit his ideas for a luxurious sleeping car to be attached to trains for long-distance travel. Pullman told a collaborating designer:

"We can make best use of the space in the car by having both lower and upper berths. But I want comfort and beauty for daytime travel, too. So, let's make the upper bunks swing down from the upper reaches of the car. If we make the lower seats face each other, they can be designed to fold down to make berths, also. All of the bunks can be surrounded by curtains to assure privacy."

So with his plan for the swing-down upper berth and a lower berth made up from two facing seats, George Pullman built a prototype car, with exterior dimensions large enough to accommodate sleeping equipment. And though the *Pioneer*, as he named his new car, was too large to clear many of the structures along the railroads, it was the most splendid land conveyance yet contrived. It was finished just in time to bear President Abraham Lincoln's body from Chicago to Springfield, with the ensuing publicity carefully nurtured by the creative Mr. Pullman.

For the next quarter century Pullman designed, modified and built all kinds of railroad cars and running gear, with the Pullman Company expanding until it was the largest manufacturing concern in the country before the end of the last century. In 1889, a Denver newspaper lavishly praised Pullman, saying:

"Had George Pullman not been a pioneer here in Colorado, the world today would have had no sleeping cars, no bathrooms, no luxurious beds, no eating rooms, but we should have travelled in the old-fashioned way—sprawling out over each other on those hot, long nights on ordinary seats, snoring and choking in dirty, old-fashioned cars, cursing in the morning for our early dawn, and swearing and damning all day at railroad travel the world over."

Perhaps so—but it seems reasonable to assume that the demand for comfort sooner or later would have brought about the changes that George Pullman initiated. Yet, to this entrepreneur goes the credit for turning the most meager creature comforts of the hard-rock miner into the most luxurious comforts of the traveler, thus insuring the financial success that had eluded Pullman in the rugged hills of Colorado.

A RUTHLESS AND DASTARDLY DEED

The omnipresent wind stirred dust devils in the street as the crowd gathered for a sanctimonious occasion. It was hot, dry and the speaker, the Hon. Thomas D. Worrall, sweltered in his dark suit and high collar. Finally, sensing a restlessness in the onlookers, Worrall removed his hat, and in a firm, senatorial voice, began to read his text:

"Our rich and expressive language is too poor in which to measure our thoughts, and only those who can penetrate the utmost reaches and read the inmost emotions of the soul can realize the depth of degradation into which we have fallen."

A preacher lamenting the sin in a boom town? A politician reflecting upon the record of the opposition?

"One of the greatest pieces of iniquity ever perpetrated in the Centennial State is that just consummated by the Mayor and the City Council of South Pueblo; and today, with bowed heads, and shame settling like a quilty pall on our countenance, we meet—not to protest—but to mourn."

Now Mr. Worrall was warming to his task. This was his kind of performance. He glanced up at his audience, wiped his brow with a linen handkerchief, then continued:

"The blindness of ignorance is inexplicable; and if this alone prompted the act of which we complain, we could turn our eyes to heaven and say: 'Father, forgive them—they know not what they do.' But back of this ignorance were passions that amount to crimes—envy, hatred, malice, love of revenge, inordinate conceit, abuse of power, and tyranny. As our citizens now tramp our sidewalks and gaze upon this desolation, old men weep, strong men curse, young men wonder, and even maidens sigh."

Worrall wiped his face again, then studied the sheath of papers in his hand. He cleared his throat once, twice, and accepted a cup of water offered by a friend. Then he shook his fist, and said:

"There is something so appalling about this act of our City Council that the whole community is shocked by its audacity. Like a stunning and unexpected blow, its full force has not been realized, nor, as yet, has the depths of the damning crime been fathomed. When consciousness has been fully restored, men will shun the perpetrators of this deed as we would a den of ravenous beasts, or the hole of a deadly scorpion. In the meantime, we must wash our hands of the crime, and in the presence of the State which has been outraged, and of the Nation which has been robbed of one of its most noble objects, we must assert our own innocence and fasten the guilt alone where it belongs.

"A few men only are responsible, men who were chosen to be our servants, but who betrayed the confidence reposed in them, and did violence to the expressed will of the people; even going so far as to deny the right of petition, guaranteed to the poorest and meanest citizens, by the Constitution of the country. So far from consenting to the iniquity, our people are appalled by its magnitude and stand aghast at its contemplation. One word is found on every lip and that word is OUTRAGE!! Every woman who passes the spot around which cluster so many memories of the past casts her eyes upon the vacant space and cries shame. Men approaching shake their heads, and in modern language reiterate the voice of the Divine Lawgiver: 'Cursed be he who removeth his neighbor's landmark'."

But, even as he spoke, Mr. Worrall knew that the fault was not that of the councilmen alone. With head drooping, and voice drawn low, he continued:

"We know that it will be a difficult task to make men see that, as a people, we are not responsible for this act of our rulers. In that we elected such men to office, we are responsible, and must bear, each for himself, a portion of the disgrace. It could not, however, be just to charge the Continental army with the treason of Benedict Arnold; neither would it be just to charge the people of South Pueblo with the destruction, by the hands of traitors, of the largest and most noble tree in Colorado."

The crowd was silent.

THE PREACHIN' MAN

More than 300 gamblers were crowded into the primitive casino on a Sunday evening in 1890 in a typical boom town that had exploded into being after a gold strike. But the Rev. Mr. Joseph Gaston was undaunted as he mounted the chair of the faro dealer, and stood facing the revelers. Upon signal from the proprietor—a pistol shot—the gambling stopped, and after a few moments of awkward quieting, all turned to the man of cloth, uncovering their heads. For 15 minutes they listened to the preacher talk on the text, "If a man dies, shall he live again?"

Most of the miners and camp followers were trying to cram enough into one life to not worry about another. But they respected the preaching man's position and admired him, if not his zeal.

At the conclusion of his brief sermon, Mr. Gaston began reciting, in a low voice:

"Our Father, who art in heaven, hallowed be thy name. . . ."

The room was even more still than before. Then a voice joined in—and another:

"Thy Kingdom come, Thy will be done. . . ."

Voices raised in chorus throughout the room. Men who had not thought of these words since they left their mother's knee, decades before, clawed deep into their memories, much as they did in the beguiling rock, now seeking a vein of conscience rather than precious metal:

"In earth as it is in heaven. Give us this day our daily bread. . . ."

The room was alive with memories of Sundays past, years and years before—of small country churches, with straight, hard-backed pews; of families sitting around the table with hands clasped as they recited the words; of a graveyard in Missouri, where a chilling fog sucked warmth from the body:

"And forgive us our debts, as we forgive our debtors. . . ."

Transfixed in their momentary reverie, the men continued as the words resounded from the walls of the gaming room:

"For thine is the kingdom, and the power, and the glory, forever. AMEN."

A few drops of moisture rolled down grizzled, unshaven faces. For a moment, no one moved, or spoke, as the preacher stood silently, with head bowed.

Then, a nervous laugh, and the spell was broken. Once more the men, now relieved of the tension of the powerful words, cast their attention to the cards and the dice:

"The queen wins and the trey loses. Thirty-one on the black."

Men who had held their stacks of chips in their hands turned back to play. The preacher closed his Bible, stepped down from the chair, shook hands with the proprietor, and started out the door. From the rear of the room, someone cried out:

"Say, boys, we forgot something. Let's take up a collection for the parson. Here's my hat, and five bucks to get it started."

But the preacher turned, smiled goodnaturedly, and said:

"Thank you, my brothers, but that was not why I was here."

And with that he was gone.

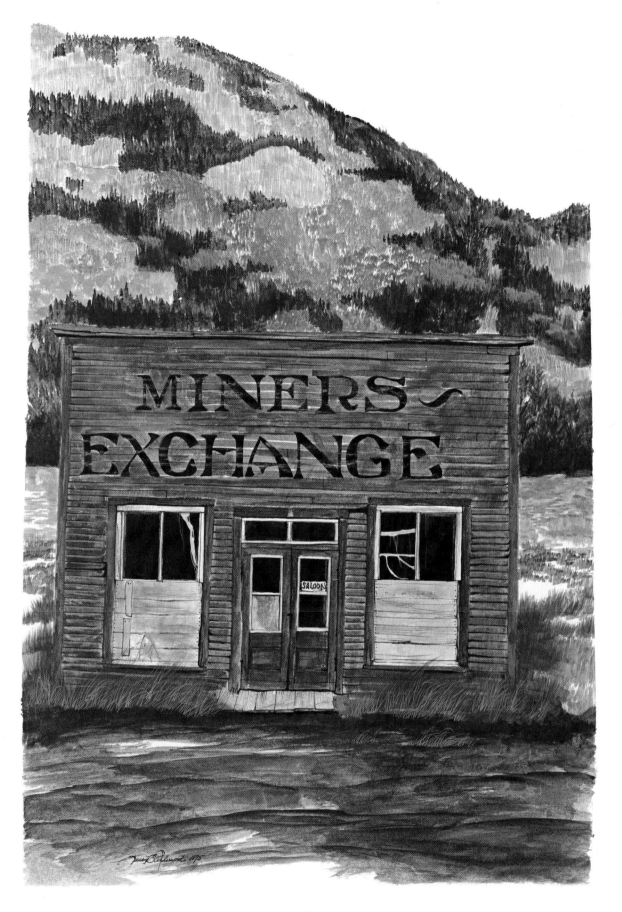

COLORADO'S FIRST TURKEY DRIVE

Late one fall in the early 1860's, Ed Rife started from Lawrence, Kansas for Denver with an oxcart of goods for trading. Amidst his other cargo were a dozen fine turkey gobblers and their rations of food. But, being inexperienced with the appetites of turkeys, Rife miscalculated the amount of food he had brought along for the birds, and before the trip was half over, the turkeys had consumed everything he carried for them. So, one evening Rife turned all twelve of the birds out of their cages, to survive or die on the prairie, depending upon their own will to live.

But, when Rife hitched up and started on the next morning, the turkeys came trailing along behind the slow-moving van, their craws full of grasshoppers and other insects they had managed to root out of the grass. For six weeks thereafter, the turkeys had no trouble keeping up with the plodding oxen.

Ed Rife's troubles with the birds came at night, however, when hungry coyotes and wolves tried to make meals of the gobblers. Though it cost him many a night's sleep, Rife did his best to protect the turkeys, even to the point of setting grass fires to ward off marauders. When he did that, Rife had to sit up to make sure the flames did not spread to his wagon or flash back on his charges.

Finally Rife reached the Mile High City, with nine of the original dozen birds, all in good flesh. There he arranged a turkey shoot on the day before Christmas, charging 25¢ a shot to the eager men who had dreams of turkey dinner for Christmas. Since most of the men of Denver were excellent shots with the rifle—and to place a proper value on birds that had been driven several hundred miles across the plains—Rife insisted that the shooters be blindfolded.

While Rife's pockets filled with coins, the area of the shoot, beside Cherry Creek, filled with the acrid smell of gunpowder. But the birds went unscathed until John Lower, the town's best marksman, got the range and direction down so well that he shot six of the gobblers. The other three were slain by accidental shots. In the tradition of dividing the spoils, Lower shared his prizes, and the turkeys were stuffed and baked in several ovens that Christmas. In the end, Ed Rife had collected about $75 for his birds, a small price to the people of Denver whose thoughts that Christmas day drifted back to childhood in their eastern homes, far away.

DAVE DAY AND *THE SOLID MULDOON*

David F. Day (the F was for Frakes, though it could have been for Fearless) must have set a record as a Colorado newspaper editor in the latter part of the last century, for at one point he had 47 libel suits pending against him.

But no claimant ever collected a cent!

As editor first of *The Solid Muldoon* and later the *Durango Democrat*, Dave Day wrote the truth as he saw it, and dared to speak his mind in a way few newspapermen ever did. As his obituary said, in 1914: "His enemies proved his sincerity and ability."

One of Colorado's two Civil War Medal of Honor winners, Day knew the men and the measures in Colorado as few persons have, and he was never afraid to tell what he knew. Rarely did readers have to wait long before learning the editor's position on matters of vital interest to southwestern Colorado or the rest of the state.

The crusty journalist began his career at Ouray, in September, 1879, when Day and a fellow Democrat, Gerald Lechter, started *The Solid Muldoon*. That name created much interest and Lechter once told how it came about:

"I had told Dave we had to give the paper a proper name. He looked around at the towering sandstone cliffs surrounding the town, thought awhile, then said; 'We want something that means solid and honest—something as solid as Bill Muldoon. That's it—we'll call it *The Solid Muldoon*.' So, that's what we named it."

Day was an admirer of William Muldoon, a sportsman and promoter of prize fights in New York City. And though the connection was obscure for most persons, *The Solid Muldoon* was by no means published in obscurity, for it quickly gained readers far beyond Ouray's mountain setting, and was one of the most widely read and quoted papers in the west. Even Queen Victoria was a subscriber.

The *Muldoon's* editor followed no set newspaper style or precepts, but was bold and defiant. From the beginning, Day attacked individuals or groups alike whenever he felt there was injustice, dishonesty, double-dealing, or any other wrongdoing. He made many enemies, but just as many friends.

Day established himself as a paragrapher, and his statements often were copied and rewritten. A fellow editor once wrote of the newspaper:

"The scene on the afternoon of *The Solid Muldoon* issue was memorable in Ouray. Copies were snatched 'hot off the press' and read aloud amid roars of laughter by men assembled in front of the rows of saloons that lined Main Street. The wit was coarse, but thoroughly genuine, and instantly became popular throughout the state and the west; especially in the camps of the San Juan mining region."

A sample of Muldoon paragraphs includes:

"God hates a coward, yet there are several of them engineering so-called newspapers."

"At prevailing prices for beef and turkeys we can see the wisdom of creating the cottontail. It is for printers, barbers, and fellows without the ability to amass as much as $4 in bulk."

Day took potshots at other communities, too, and once stimulated an exchange with *The Montrose Messenger*. Day had written:

"The owls and buzzards are negotiating for winter quarters in Montrose. It certainly will be secluded and quiet enough."

But the *Messenger* fired right back with:

"That is rough on Ourayites, David, and we never heard them called such names before—a dozen Ouray families propose wintering in Montrose the coming season."

Although David Day was a Democrat, and the *Muldoon* had been founded with money put up by others of like persuasion, Day did not always agree with the party line. This brought one Democrat to say:

"I paid $800 to get him in here, and now I'd give twice that to get rid of him."

In 1892, Day moved his family and his newspaper to Durango where he published both a daily and weekly edition. In the fall of 1893, after *The Solid Muldoon* had been merged with the *Daily Herald*, Day founded the *Durango Democrat*, which remained in the family until a few years after the editor's death in 1914.

Long after David Day had passed from the scene, the press used for his newspaper at Ouray was still hard at work, and until about 1960 it was used to publish the *Silverton Standard*.

It still was called *"The Solid Muldoon."*

THE ORPHAN PEAK

Ten miles north of Walsenburg, on a bank of the Huerfano River, is a 250-foot pile of jagged rock that was a prominent point in southern Colorado history long before Zebulon Pike sighted the lofty neighbor to the north that is so much better known.

Tiny Huerfano Peak—El Huerfano, as the Spanish explorers called it—is a cone-shaped mound, removed from other hills or peaks, and is, therefore, an "Orphan."

Echoes of iron-shod horse hoofs and the clanging of swords reportedly were heard by Indians who gathered pinon nuts near the peak in 1540 when Coronado and his expedition passed through the eastern section of what is now Huerfano County. Spanish settlers moved into the area long before the landing of the pilgrims at Plymouth Rock, and crude crosses, indicating their final resting place, have been found with dates back as far as 1581.

Even though "El Huerfano" was established in the annals of the earliest Spanish adventurers in Colorado, this montane midget, so steeped in history, is clothed in obscurity in the land where the mountains are a family of giants.

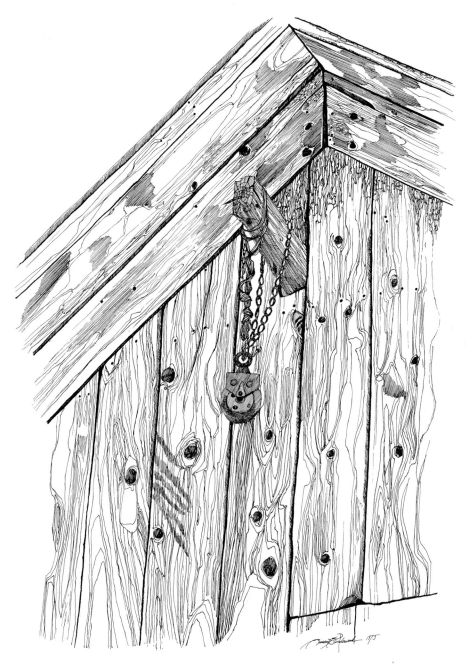

TO BE WITH HIS KIND

"Sam, I don't think I've seen you so purtied up since you come to Cripple Creek."

"Well, it isn't every day that a man loses his best friend. We've been together ever since St. Joe . . . crossed the plains, lived high off the hog and have starved together. He never let me down. Yes sir, ol' Sandy never let me down."

"That's a fine-looking casket. Real fine lookin'!"

"Yup. He never lifted his leg on a better one."

"When's the funeral?"

"Oh, folks will be gatherin' soon."

"Going to bury him out with the others?"

"Sure, I think he ought to be with his kind in the end."

Sandy had been one of the better known dogs in Cripple Creek. He had no special blood lines, but had inherited the capacities for love and loyalty that now were being rewarded on his passing. More than 100 men gathered for the funeral procession from the Colorado Hotel to the regular plot of ground set aside for pet burial. A wealthy miner had bequeathed $100 for proper maintenance of the canine cemetery.

Funerals for dogs of the miners who had struck it rich were practically state occasions. They often began and ended with no small consumption of distilled spirits, and somewhere in between rounds of the bottle the remains of the departed friend were transported to the cemetery. This did not change even after cars appeared in Cripple Creek. In fact, one rich miner, angered because he could not get the services of the new motor-driven hearse in Cripple Creek, chartered all the cars in town for the procession to the dog cemetery. The body of the dog was placed in the lead vehicle, and other cars solemnly followed along behind.

Yes, for Sandy and Spike, Ranger and Duke—all the good ol' boys of dogdom—dignity was a fact of death in Cripple Creek.

THE SARTORIALLY-SELECT SCHOOLMAN

It required marvelous courage to conduct a school in Denver in 1859, a courage that few men possessed. For the most part, the Mile High City was awash with adventurers, gold hunters who had flocked there in search of their personal fortune. They also sought the riches of the flesh, not the wealth of the soul that book-learning might bring.

But, despite great odds against success, a strong and willful man began the work that was the prelude for a fine public school system in Denver, and recognition for Colorado as a state with exceptional educational leadership. That man was O. J. Goldrick. Born in Ireland and educated at Trinity, Goldrick first lived in Ohio after moving to the United States, where he combined the unlikely professions of book seller and hog raiser. He also wrote poetry, when he wasn't looking after his livestock. But when the fabulous stories of the new gold mines in Colorado spread over the country, Goldrick was smitten with the age-old dream of riches and came west by oxcart.

It is not clear just when he decided that Denver needed to be educated. It may have been his first day in the raucous town, when Mr. Goldrick stepped into the street wearing a high, stove-pipe hat and frock coat. The Irishman immediately was looked upon as a joke, and was compelled to submit to a hazing he never forgot. One old miner said:

"Well, now, ain't he the dandy, though. Bet one shot from ol' Betsy 'd have him heading east agin faster'n those mangy oxen ever moved 'fore."

In the next few days, old army pistols were taken out, loaded and primed, while their owners waited for a chance for a pot-shot at the shining hat, which Goldrick brushed carefully each day. And more than one youngster was restrained by an anxious mother from letting fly a rock or mud-ball at the inviting target.

But O. J. Goldrick was undaunted. In fact, he seemed to thrive on the attention, and rather than submit to the derision of his fellow men, he exercised a tonsorial selection that only added to the eccentricities of his character, which became fabled. Goldrick had the courage to fully support his own conviction. And since he thought everything depended upon education, and was a born pedagogue, he soon opened Colorado's first school, on Ferry Street in "Auraria," now West Denver. The school building was a rented log house, with a dirt floor, and Goldrick charged a tuition of $3 a month for the 13 students whose character he was given to mold.

Since the high hat and long coat were part of the professor's daily attire, his hazers soon tired of their treatment of Goldrick and allowed him to walk along the streets of the frontier town unmolested. In fact, out of their original scorn for the plucky Irishman came admiration for Goldrick as an institution, a person of cool nerve and grit, who believed strongly and expressed himself to his beliefs. And for the next quarter of a century he generally was regarded as the best dressed gentleman in all of the mountain states.

In addition to the courage which Goldrick showed on many occasions, he was known afar for his jovial spirit and his quick repartee. His writings displayed his eccentricities, though he always was original, and at times was brilliantly eloquent.

Even on his death bed, Goldrick's humor never left him. A few hours before his passing, he had a request:

"Bring me a barber, that I may make a presentable appearance. No pig-scraper, but an artist, one who can hold his razor and his tongue at the same time."

Thus Colorado's first educator died with a smoothly shaved face, and a trail of memories that followed him into the grave.

THERE WAS NO NIGHT IN CREEDE
"HOLY MOSES!"

Some say this was the exclamation of a surprised Nicholas Creede when he received the assay results of ore taken from Campbell Mountain in southwestern Colorado in the early fall of 1890.

Other reports are that the reaction came when a frustrated Creede, pausing to rest for lunch, smashed his pick into the earth, and then realized he had hit pay dirt.

Whichever is correct—and both may be—the *Holy Moses* mine began a rush to the San Juans that for a short period in the early 1890's outpaced even Cripple Creek, which was burgeoning at the same time.

Prospectors, miners, saloon keepers, cardsharks, prostitutes, merchandisers pushed into the narrow valley of Willow Creek, and, under walls that rise a thousand feet, built shacks, stores, rooming houses and saloons on every bit of reasonably level ground and even over the creek.

Cy Warman, colorful editor of the *Creede Chronicle*, captured life in the boom town with a simple verse:

"It's day all day in the daytime
And there is no night in Creede."

Creede produced a good sum of wealth for a period, though in comparison to the major gold camps of Central City and Cripple Creek, the total was small. Yet the town provided this saying:

"Don't jostle that fellow! He may be a millionaire tomorrow and resent the insult."

Creede attracted all kinds. One of the less desirable citizens was Robert Ford, a barkeep who had opened a dance hall at the corner of San Luis Avenue and Second Street. Ford had a singular notoriety: he had killed Jesse James, though the manner of the execution of the bad man brought more disdain for Ford than glory.

At frequent intervals, Ford would insulate his courage with redeye, then venture out to shoot up the town. On several occasions he compelled people spending a quiet evening on the Rialto, Creede's main street, to duck for cover. These forays would bring admonishment from the *Chronicle*, to which Ford would issue threats to kill everyone connected with the paper from the editor and poet laureate to the copy boy. Fortunately, Ford never made good his threats.

But Robert Ford knew his life was as uncertain as the many ore veins that followed the fissures in the dense rock walls of Willow Creek. When he drank at the bar of his saloon, his eyes slid back and forth rapidly around the room, and to the mirror behind the bar. As a back shooter, he knew the dangers of relaxation.

Yet, despite his precautions, Robert Ford was gunned down by a fellow saloon keeper, a man named Red Kelley, who felt he not only would do the town a public service but would earn himself a reputation by shooting Ford. Kelley selected a shotgun for the task, and on a Sunday evening, slipped into Ford's dance hall where Ford was in front of the bar.

"Oh, Bob!" he called. Ford intuitively reached for his gun as he turned toward the door, but Kelley fired both barrels at close range, killing Ford instantly.

Kelley achieved fame of a sort. He was tried, convicted, and sentenced to life in the penitentiary.

The funeral services for Robert Ford never would be seen as the social high mark of the early days of Creede. They were held in a storeroom, which happened to be vacant at the time, and the preacher experienced difficulty finding something good to say about him, considering Bob's record. But the man of cloth did the best he could under the circumstances.

Ford was interred in the rustic cemetery on the side of a hill, not far from the grave of Slanting Annie, a lady of the night whose unfortunate life ended shortly after she joined the rush to Creede. But Ford's remains were later removed to Missouri by his wife, who had stayed behind in the border state.

Creede grew to nearly 10,000 people at one time, with men living under the most incredible conditions. But the miners moved on almost as fast as they came when they realized that the original predictions for the area were exaggerated. Nicholas Creede reportedly sold the Holy Moses mine for $70,000, a tidy figure for the times, but far under the wealth of which he dreamed.

MOUNTAIN CHARLIE

To his friends he was known as Mountain Charlie—trapper, Indian fighter and mountain man. But to the world he was Charles Stewart Stobie, one of the most talented artists to put the life of early Colorado to the test of the paint brush.

Stobie, in the tradition of Charlie Russell and Frederic Remington—the latter a friend—"lived" the scenes that he later applied to canvas. He painted cowboys on the range and in camp, glorious landscapes, and Indian battles, all from observation. Stobie also was an accomplished portraitist, and is remembered for his studies of Kit Carson, Sitting Bull, Standing Bear, Black Bear, Little Wolf, Buffalo Bill and other Indians and military figures with whom he lived and worked.

Mountain Charlie was born in Baltimore on March 18, 1845. His family moved west—to Chicago—when he was about 18 years old, and the restless young painter crossed the plains to Colorado in 1865, when he was just 20 years old. It was on that trip that Stobie was introduced to warring Indians, for his wagon train was attacked three times between Fort Sedgwick and Fort Kearney. Stobie became an instant hero upon his arrival in Denver when it was noted publicly that he had personally killed seven Indians.

Stobie quickly adopted the dress and life of the mountain men, and his mentors were some of the most famous to leave a trail in Colorado—Jim Baker, Kit Carson, James Beckwourth, and others. Amused by his skill with the sketchpad, Carson once told him:

"Charlie, you'd better spend more time learning to use the knife and gun as well as you do the pencil, or you won't keep your top thatch long enough to become a famous painter."

But Mountain Charlie did learn fast, and since he preferred the companionship of Carson and others, he fast became skilled in the independent life in buckskins. And, he always credited both his introduction and liking to that life and the success he attained in the west to the advice and example of the more experienced men.

Despite his bloody introduction to the plains Indians, Stobie became friendly with the mountain tribes, especially the Utes. Stobie lived with Nevada's Ute band in 1866, and was the only white man with the Ute war party that fought with the Arapahoes and Cheyennes in Middle Park. Upon return to the main village, Pagh-agh-et (Long Hair), as Stobie was called, took part in the scalp dances and victory celebration that lasted almost two weeks. To the Utes he was a warrior who had fulfilled his mission in life.

As a scout and buffalo hunter operating out of the White River Ute Agency, Stobie made many trips into Wyoming to the north, and south to the borders of New Mexico and Arizona. He became well known to many bands of Indians he met in his travels, and was one of those who early explored the cliff dwellings at Mesa Verde.

Stobie returned to Chicago for the late years of his life, where he died in August, 1931, approaching the age of 86. He had learned well in Colorado.

OURAY, THE MEDIATOR

Some say his name meant "Arrow." Others believe it was the Ute word (Oo-ya) for "yes." The man himself said the name had no special meaning, but was what his Ute father and Apache mother called him as a child.

He was Ouray, great chief of the Ute nation, and one of the most remarkable leaders among men the west has known.

Short in stature, long in brilliance, Ouray was a man of vision and wisdom, who had experienced a cross-cultured life. He spoke Spanish and understood English in addition to several Indian dialects. He also understood the ways of the white man, who came into his lands, and he once questioned:

"Is the government of the United States not strong enough to keep its treaties?"

Ouray probably was the most influential friend the white invaders had among the Colorado Indians throughout the period referred to as the Indian Uprisings. The chief wanted peace, but he also wanted fair treatment of his people. He tried, desperately, to control the Utes while upholding terms of a series of useless treaties signed with his nation.

But Ouray saw each successive effort fail, as more land was franchised to the whites, and more abuses fell upon the remaining territory. Yet, time and again, Ouray led or sent warriors and messengers into the field to stop his own people, and on more than one occasion he warned settlers of impending attacks when he could not control hostile war chiefs.

Ouray was one of the first Utes to attempt a life of ranching, partly because he recognized that the nomadic freedom of the Utes through their wide domain was changing, but also because he wanted to set an example for the others of the nation. Yet, even as he was bringing brood animals to his ranch in the Uncompahgre Valley, white miners and stock growers were invading the ore-rich and grassy San Juans, in violation of the treaty that had been brought about through great personal effort of Ouray.

In 1872, Washington ordered a council to meet at the Los Pinos Indian Agency in southwestern Colorado to try to induce the Utes to cede the San Juans to the United States. Once again Ouray was the central figure in the negotiations. Only this time, instead of being the mediator and conciliator, the chief calmly and brilliantly analyzed and countered every proposition put forth by the government commissioners. Then he rose, and with dignity and eloquence, demolished each point on the commissioner's pre-arranged list, and shamed them by exposing violations of pledges and willful attempts to nullify a contract that had been formulated and ratified by the Senate of the United States.

But, Ouray had as much chance stopping those who waited to swarm upon the Ute lands as a lightening rod has of stopping an electrical storm. He could only attempt to minimize the despoilment for his people.

Fortunately, Ouray did not live to see the final disgrace heaped upon the Utes, who finally were ousted from their lands and marched to the Uintah Reservation in neighboring Utah. For, indeed it would merely have proved to the chief that the United States was strong enough *not* to keep its treaties.

THE PRIDE OF LAKE CITY

"He was a gentle soul, quiet and kindly. All the children loved him like a grandfather. It's hard to believe all those stories about him."

Such were the comments about Alferd Packer when he was laid to rest in a hillside cemetery at Littleton on April 23, 1907. But the death of Packer wrote the concluding chapter of one of the most grotesque tales of mountain history, for the quiet man whom the children loved was a convicted murderer—and a confessed cannibal.

Alferd Packer was the only man ever tried in the United States on a charge of cannibalism, and the "Maneater," as he came to be called, was convicted in two separate trials, on little material evidence. That he subsisted on the bodies of fellow men is not to be denied, but the question of whether or not he was a murderer is less clear.

The story of Alferd Packer begins as did many others in the formative days of Colorado, on a prospecting expedition. Packer was one of 21 men who set out from Utah to seek gold in the mountains near Breckinridge, Colorado. Alferd Packer served as their guide.

Once on the way, severe weather threatened the party, and delays in their travel cut food rations, so that when they entered the Uncompahgre River Valley in late January, 1874, they were living on their horses' feed. Surprised by a band of Ute Indians, the prospectors were taken to the camp of Chief Ouray, at the confluence of the Gunnison and Uncompahgre River, where they were well treated while they waited for better weather.

Days, then weeks, went by, and the men grew impatient, as the desire for riches sounded a golden flute in their minds. Finally, on February 8, 1874, six men under the leadership of Packer set out once again for Breckenridge, despite severe storm warnings. Packer's companions were young George Noon, Shannon Bell, Frank Miller, James Humphreys, and 60-some years old Israel Swan.

What happened the next 66 days was known only to Alferd Packer, who may have taken full knowledge to his grave. But, on April 16, a bewhiskered and half-starved Packer dragged himself into the Los Pinos Indian Agency, the sole survivor of the group. Packer said he had become snowblind, and that the others had left him behind, but that he had found his way out. No one questioned his story, even though he had Swan's rifle and Miller's knife.

Once recovered, Packer moved on to Saguache, still trying to get to Breckinridge. In Saguache, Packer became a steady visitor to the saloon of Larry Dolan, and he seemed to have a considerable amount of money, despite his claims to be poor. Other members of the original party of 21 had reached Saguache now, and as Dolan's liquor brought forth differing versions of Packer's adventure, they became suspicious of him, and insisted he be questioned once again.

Now, under direct questioning by General Charles Adams, the Indian agent at Los Pinos, Alferd Packer made his first confession.

He told how the party had run out of supplies, and that no game was available to them for food. Swan, the oldest of the group, died of starvation, Packer said, and the remaining men boiled his flesh to survive. Several days later, when Humphreys died, the survivors again shared his remains, as they did when Miller died sometime later. Packer claimed Bell shot Noon, adding the young man's body to their larder, and that Bell tried to shoot him, but missed. Packer said he then killed Bell, in self defense, with his hatchet. He signed this confession on May 8, 1847 and was immediately jailed in Saguache, for suspected homicide.

A break in the bizarre case came the following August, when the skeletal remains of Packer's five companions were accidentally discovered on a bluff overlooking what now is Lake City, Colorado. All five skulls had deep splits, as if caused by a hatchet, and other facts contradicted Packer's signed confession. Though Packer then was put in irons, he escaped and was a free man until he was recognized by another of the original 21 at a roadhouse in Wyoming nine years later. Arrested without incident, Packer was returned to Colorado, where he now told another story.

Now Packer said that the group had run out of food shortly after leaving the camp of Chief Ouray, and had blundered on until trapped by a snow storm. Unable to find food, they even boiled their moccasins for food. One day, Packer said, he was out of camp, and when he returned, Bell was roasting a piece of meat at the fire. Bell attacked him with a hatchet, and Packer had to shoot him. Then, Packer claimed, he found the bodies of the other four prospectors, all killed by hatchet blows to the head. Packer said he had to remain in camp for 60 some days because of the deep snow, and that he lived off the flesh of his companions during that period. Finally he was able to get out to the Los Pinos Agency.

Alferd Packer was brought to trial for murder on April 9, 1883, in the Lake City Courthouse. The jury did not believe his story, and reached a verdict in only three hours: guilty. They believed robbery to be the motive. Packer was sentenced to hang.

The verdict and sentence spawned a colorful—but inaccurate—legend in Lake City. One man ran from the courtroom to the saloon, where he quoted Judge Melville Gerry as saying:

"There was only seven Democrats in Hinsdale County and you, you voracious man-eating S.O.B., you ate five of 'em. I sentence you to hang."

Packer escaped the noose because of a legal technicality in which he could not be legally sentenced to hang, under a revision of Colorado law that had taken place in 1881. He was granted a retrial, this time at Gunnison, where he was charged and convicted on five counts of manslaughter, and sentenced to 40 years in the Colorado State Penitentiary at Canon City.

Packer was a model prisoner at Canon City, where he studied about plants and became an expert gardener. As time passed, the public revulsion for him faded, replaced by sympathy. Petitions were circulated for his release, supported by the penitentiary warden, newspapers, and influential private citizens. One of the last acts in office by Gov. Charles S. Thomas was to grant the 59 year old Packer a conditional release from prison in January of 1901.

Alferd Packer moved to the Denver area, where he prospected for copper and made friends with his neighbors, and especially the children. He suffered a stroke in July, 1906, and was nursed by friends until he died on April 23, 1907.

Grotesque as the story of Alferd Packer is, it generated a local pride of sorts. In a 1930 newspaper column, Will Rogers told a brief story of Packer, noting that he was tried and convicted at Del Norte. This angered the proud citizens of Lake City, and prompted an editorial in the Lake City *Silver World* that said:

"Lake City is threatened with the loss of much of that on which its glory is founded . . . we know the Packer case from Dan to Beer-Sheba. It belongs to Lake City, not Del Norte, nor Gunnison, and they and all others are warned to keep off the grass."

A marker was placed on Cannibal Plateau, outside Lake City, noting the spot where Packer's companions were found. And today, the Alferd Packer Feasting and Friendship Society is headquartered in Lake City. This public-spirited group has the slogan, "Serving Our Fellow Man Since 1875."

THE KIOWA CREEK LOCOMOTIVE

Late in the afternoon of May 21, 1878, a storm gathered in the mountains west of Palmer Lake, then moved rapidly along the crest of the Front Range and east from the hills.

For more than an hour a cloudburst dropped the heaviest rain in the region of the eastern plains that anyone living there could remember. One old settler said:

"Never seen it rain like this, 'cept maybe in the big flood of '64. But you watch out. We're in for trouble 'fore this storm is over."

And he was right. Cherry, Box Elder, Bijou and Kiowa Creeks all rose rapidly and torrents of water sloshed over the banks. The flood hit Denver about midnight, washing out bridges and sweeping away telegraph poles.

At 10:30 p.m., a freight train belonging to the Kansas Pacific Railroad left Denver, bound for Kansas City. Though running in heavy rain, Engineer John Bacon was unaware of any need for special precautions, for the train had departed Denver before the flood waters hit the city. But, at the section house at Kiowa Creek, the roar of the swollen waterway woke up the foreman, who rushed to the bridge just in time to see it give way to the pressure of the flood. And above the noise of the flood, the foreman barely heard the whistle of the approaching locomotive, across the creek, and still some distance from the destroyed bridge.

"My God! The night freight . . . I've got to warn them."

But, as he was running for a red lantern, the light of the locomotive pierced the mist, then disappeared as the engine and several cars plunged into the swirling waters.

The next day, a work train was sent from Deertrail to look for the train, now reported missing. The engineer of the work train later reported:

"A message was sent to Kansas City and back to Deertrail. We were told to 'Flag west' and look for No. 8. We took the engine and one flatcar and started to look for the missing train. About a half mile from Kiowa Creek, we flagged through a cut, and I saw the trestle down, the train in the river, but no engine. Down the stream, lodged in the trees, was the caboose, and with it were two bums who told us about the accident. The engine of No. 8 had fallen into a bed of quicksand that was 53 feet deep, and was so completely covered up that no trace was ever found of it."

Engineer Bacon, his fireman, Frank Seldon, and John Piatt, a brakeman, all went down with the engine. Two bodies were recovered the day after the accident about two miles downstream, and the third was found later about 10 miles below the accident site. All of the bodies bore injuries received in the crash, indicating that death most likely had been instantaneous.

Search for the missing engine began a few days after burial of the victims, and following the construction of a temporary track around the gap. The sand was probed with long metallic rods, and pits were started in some places, but abandoned because of heavy underflow. Finally, the $18,000 locomotive was deserted, left in its sandy tomb.

In the nearly hundred years that have passed since the train plunged into Kiowa Creek, instruments have been developed that might locate a large mass of metal beneath the bed of the waterflow. But, most likely, the location of No. 8 will remain an unsolved mystery of the Colorado plains.

HORACE TABOR'S TOO-SMALL HOUSE

Children began lining up for the matinee performance of *H.M.S. Pinafore* long before the doors of the magnificent Tabor Opera House in Denver were to open. By 1 p.m., Sixteenth Street from Curtis to Arapahoe, was a mass of restless youngsters, and a cacophony of excitement. Traffic had stopped. Trolleys were unable to get in and out of the car barn, and patrons to the post office decided their letters could wait, rather than venture through the writhing energy.

All efforts to keep the children quiet were wasted, and most adults who saw the eagerness with which the youngsters awaited the performance only smiled, with knowing remembrances.

Jim Lomery, Denver's likable chief of police, came down the street, a resplendent figure in his gold-braided military hat, shining brass buttons, and striped pants. Lomery tried to quiet the children, and for a few moments held their attention. As he waved his hat to command silence and attention, a kid hollered:

"Say, Mister, if you're the captain of the Pinafore, cheese the jaw boning and get back on stage."

The genial Lomery howled approval along with the children.

Finally, the great doors to the house were opened, and the children streamed into the opera house, now becoming quiet in their awe of its splendor. Forty-two children alone were in the Tabor box, and all seats and standing room were filled.

But for one little girl, there would be no matinee performance that afternoon. Huddled against the Curtis Street door of the opera house, she sobbed and sobbed, as only a heart-broken child can cry.

A kindly gentleman, who had circled around to Curtis Street from the Sixteen Street entrance, which was jammed with youngsters, leaned down to comfort her and said:

"Here, little lady, what is this all about?"

"I . . . I want to go to the program," she sobbed, "but there's no more room."

"Now, now, my dear. It is so crowded with other children like you, that even I can't get in. Do you know who I am?"

Through eyes fogged with tears the child looked at the tall man, who had piercing black eyes, and a drooping flared mustache.

"No, I don't know who you are. And it doesn't matter anyway."

"Well, now, maybe it does. I am Horace Tabor and I own this building. But even I can't get in today."

The small head cocked to one side, and the mask of sorrow changed to disdain:

"Are you Senator Tabor?"

"Yes, child, I am."

"And you built this opera house?"

"Yes, I did."

"And it won't hold one more person?"

"No, my dear, not even one more little girl."

"Well," she said, defiantly, "If I were you and I couldn't build an opera house that would hold all the children in town, I'd go back to Leadville and crawl in a mine and stay there."

Later, when he told the story, Horace Tabor said:

"Right then and there, all pride in the opera house was gone."

But though a little girl could not get in the matinee performance of *Pinafore* that memorable day in the 1880's, she had the finest seat in the house for the final performance of the company that evening. And nearby was the former Senator from Colorado, who tended her every wish, like a doting manservant to an appreciative princess.

THE PICKETWIRE

Contrary to popular belief that the Purgatoire River received its name because of the region upon which it trespasses before joining the Arkansas east of Las Animas, the "Picketwire," as it sometimes has been called, supports evidence of very early explorations into Colorado by Spanish expeditionary forces.

The river has appeared on old maps of Colorado as "The Animas," the "Las Animas," "Purgatory," and the "Purgatoire." Some early maps refer to it as "El Rio de Las Animas Perdidas en Purgatorio."

While early Spanish-speaking residents of southern Colorado reportedly used the full name of the river, French trappers operating out of Bent's Fort applied the name "Purgatoire." Early English stockmen in the area accepted the French name, but unaccustomed to the French tongue, assumed the name to have something to do with staking out a horse, and thereby called it "Picketwire"—the way they heard the name from the trappers.

Writing in a 1928 issue of *The Colorado Magazine*, Judge A. W. McHendrie of Trinidad detailed the naming of the river, and associated it with a Spanish expedition that watered in the area in the late 1500's, most likely the first non-Indian visitors to Colorado. McHendrie fixes the date at between 1595 and 1596, when the forces of Captain Francisco Leiva Bonilla were sent out by the Spanish governor of Nueva Biscaya to suppress war-like tribes in the northern part of his province. When his mission was accomplished, Captain Bonilla, a native of Portugal, continued north into the lands of New Mexico, seeking the legendary golden city of Quivira. When the governor of Nueva Biscaya learned that the expedition had gone further than permitted, he sent a Spanish officer to overtake Bonilla, with orders to return at once to Nueva Biscaya. However, Captain Bonilla disregarded the orders, and continued north, although some of his men refused to follow him and returned to Old Mexico.

Shortly after that Captain Bonilla fought with his second in command, a Spanish officer named Juan de Humana, and Bonilla was killed. At that point, the Spanish priests who accompanied the party—not only by custom but by regulation—considered their new leader a murderer and would no longer continue on what they considered a cursed mission.

On their return, the Spanish soldiers were confronted and killed by massed Indians along the banks of a then unnamed river north of what is now the border between Colorado and New Mexico. Remnants of rusted weapons and armor were discovered by another Spanish expedition in November, 1598. Padres with the second party, knowing that the priests had not been with the Bonilla-Humana party when attacked, quickly dubbed this tributary to the Arkansas "El Rio de Las Animas Perdidas en Purgatorio"—"the river of the souls lost in Purgatory."

Perhaps they are held there by a picketwire.

50

COLORFUL TAHOSA?

It could have been "Idahoe"—gem of the mountains. Or "Tampa," "San Juan," "Lulu" or even "Nemara."

"Arapahoe," following the name of a tribe of Indians that inhabited the region also was a popular name for the new territory among those considered by the United States Senate in 1860, as reported in the *Rocky Mountain News.* "Colarado" (sic) was being considered, too.

The territory initially had been called "Jefferson," but the legislators reasoned that there were not enough presidents to affix their names to all future states. Besides, Washington "stood alone in his glory."

While the Senators were debating the name, a House of Representatives committee, rejected "Weapollea" and had settled on "Tahosa," meaning "dweller of the mountain tops." Speculation ran high that "Tahosa" or "Idahoe" would be selected.

But "Colorful Tahosa?" "Glory, glory Jefferson?" No—never!

The melodious Indian names and other titles were rejected by the law makers, who finally settled on Colorado, the Spanish word for red, which had been attached first to the great river that rises in the Continental Divide and flows to the Gulf of California.

THE PREVARICATOR OF PIKE'S PEAK

Few military outposts were as desolate as the weather and signal station established atop Pike's Peak in the early 1870's, where the personnel sometimes went weeks at a time snowbound in their tiny quarters.

For at least one man assigned to the station, the result of such isolation was madness. But for another, Sgt. John T. O'Keefe, United States Signal Corps, it was a madness of the madcap variety, and development of a reputation that reached across the land.

Sgt. O'Keefe first made headlines in May, 1876 with a gruesome story about wild mountain rats that had attacked him and his wife, and had devoured their two-month old baby. As O'Keefe's account said:

"These animals are known to feed upon a saccharine gum that percolates through the pores of the rocks apparently upheaved by that volcanic action which at irregular intervals of a few days gives the mountain crust that vibratory motion which has been detected by the instruments used in the office of the United States Signal Station."

The small detail that Pike's Peak is not of volcanic nature didn't deter O'Keefe, nor did it stop newspapers from all over the west using his story. And, in due time, a grave appeared on the mountain top, reportedly that of Erin O'Keefe. Many visitors to the mountain's lofty heights were anxious to see both the grave and the voracious rats.

O'Keefe, on another occasion, reported that he was unable to return to his station on the mountain because so little snow had fallen that he was unprepared for the obstacles he now found in the path of his climb which usually were covered with winter's crest. On a second attempt he was attacked by "six ravenous mountain lions" and he and his faithful mule, Balaam, were saved only when O'Keefe cast to the lions the seventeen mule deer which he had shot and was packing up the mountain to provide food for the winter.

Volcanic activity on the mountain was a favorite subject for the sergeant's fertile imagination. In 1880, O'Keefe reported (and the newspapers duly printed) that he was "aroused from his slumbers by a dreary, doleful sound which apparently emanated from beneath the signal station. His first impressions were that it was an earthquake, but this impression was soon dispelled by the fact that the sounds still continued without any signs of a jar."

O'Keefe reported that he and his assistant, F. L. Jones, investigated, and were greeted by a great flash of light at the summit of the peak. But then the sound subsided. Yet, when he looked further the next day, he found a crater filled with ashes and lava "which had been emitted from what he believed to be an incipient volcano." (O'Keefe's reports were filed and reported in the third person.) The sergeant noted that snow had entirely disappeared for a distance of half a mile from the crater.

Not satisfied with just one eruption, the 24-year-old O'Keefe reported a second and more violent eruption on Nov. 7, 1880. A newspaper account said:

"Sergeant O'Keefe happened to be up on the roof of the signal station on this occasion and he portrays the majesty of the scene as the grandest that he had ever witnessed, not excepting that of Vesuvius, seen by him in 1822 when he was a lad and before he left his native Italy for America."

O'Keefe had expressed concern for the safety of Colorado Springs, in that the lava from the eruption was heading for the town's water supply. And, he predicted, if the eruptions continued, no doubt "Colorado Springs would meet the same fate as that which destroyed the flourishing cities of Pompeii and Herculanem."

There was little sign of hope, according to O'Keefe:

"Scientists give it as their opinion that the present upheaval will last about three months, after which the volcano will settle down to a state of comparative repose, only to burst with renewed vigor in about six years."

One Denver newspaper reported the story had no foundation in fact, while another properly noted that O'Keefe was born in Ireland, not Italy. But, Sgt. O'Keefe would "in due time answer these imputations on the accuracy of his story."

The subject of many of O'Keefe's yarns was Balaam, the government mule that for years packed both men and supplies to the mountain top. Balaam, according to O'Keefe, was the first mule to climb the Pike's Peak trail, and also the first in history to "breathe the breath of life at an altitude of 14,400 above the level of the sea."

O'Keefe carefully recorded statistics about the mule (he claimed), and one time told reporters in Colorado Springs that in seven years Balaam had made "1,924 trips from this city to the peak, or the equivalent of 40,960 miles or about twice the circumference of the globe. He has worn out 560 sets of shoes, equal in weight to about a ton. It has cost the department to keep him during that time, including forage, shoeing and other necessary expense, somewhat over $40,000."

O'Keefe had a variety of adventures on the mountain. At one point, he reported he had smoked ten pounds of gunpowder tea when his usual ration of tobacco failed to arrive from Washington.

Such stories made John O'Keefe a hero of national stature, and when he retired from duty on Pike's Peak, he was honored by a banquet in Colorado Springs, where he was endowed with the title "Prevaricator of Pike's Peak." O'Keefe left military service, and after working some time as a telegrapher and mail agent in Denver, apparently was employed as an engine stoker with the Denver Fire Department. He died suddenly at the age of 39.

SUPERSTITIONS

Early Coloradans, like other people, had certain superstitions that they paid attention to, often based on their background or particular profession. For instance, some of the trappers in Lake County dropped a part of the animal they had caught back in the stream or lake so that there would be some remains for the ghost.

At the same time, farmers never left a rifle lying on the ground, for to step over the barrel was to bring a death in the family. Some farmers also believed that the fortunes of a family could be predicted by the way a chicken would run after its head had been cut off. If the chicken ran to the north, the result would be a death in the family. However, if it ran south, good luck would be the result.

Birds figured in still other ways in the early beliefs. Some of the mountain men believed that the eagle was the only bird that could look at the sun. And if a wild bird flew into the house, death was to occur within a week.

Of course, the mountain men also told stories of seeing hoop snakes, too. This was a snake which, if in a hurry, simply put its tail in its mouth and rolled like a hoop. Snakes were weather predictors, too: if a lot of snakes were about, there was going to be a flood. Also, you had to be careful not to place horse hairs on the surface of a water tank or horse trough, because they would turn into snakes at the next full moon.

Miners had many beliefs that governed their lives. For one thing, it was considered extremely bad luck to start a mining project on a Monday afternoon or on a Friday morning. Also, new clothes should never be worn in the mines, nor should a match be lit underground.

Mules and rats had significance in the mine. Many miners believed that mules would warn of danger in the mine, but if the rats were leaving—as they might a ship—get out, danger was at hand.

Speaking of mules—some of the miners used to claim that a mean mule was just a reincarnated foreman. Or was it the opposite?

Death supposedly came in threes at the gold mines. If an accident killed one man, sometimes the rest of the crew stayed away, feeling it wasn't safe to work until two more men had died.

The weather did—and does—still figure in many beliefs and superstitions, not all of which are without some basis in scientific fact. But it is doubtful that thunder makes milk sour and eggs spoil, as some housewives on the eastern Colorado plains once believed.

Naturally, storms could be easily predicted by the homesteaders. All they had to do was look at the moon. If they saw the face of the old man in the new moon, there would be a storm. And rings around the moon means a storm, almost always snow. The bigger the rings, the bigger the storm.

"At two o'clock in the afternoon I thought I could distinguish a mountain to our right, which appeared like a small blue cloud; viewed it with the spy-glass, and was still more confirmed in my conjecture. . . ."

Lt. Zebulon Pike
November 15, 1806

Susan B. Underwood 1975

WILLIAM T. WILLIAMS, M.T.

"Say, ain't you Bill Williams?"

"Sir, I am William T. Williams, M.T., and I would take it kindly if you would not forget that."

"Well, all right, *Mr.* William T. Williams, M.T., have it your way. But ya shore look like Bill Williams—an' ya shore *smell* like Bill Williams!"

William T. Williams, M.T.—the M.T. stood for Master Trapper—never claimed to be sure how he came to the Rockies. He told one interviewer that he "rolled out of a thunder storm in the mountains." Williams was convinced that he was not human, that he had been transformed from the Great Bear, or some other celestial animal, and put on earth for a special purpose that would be made known to him in the hereafter.

Some of his fellow trappers and guides believed Williams, while others took his claims in stride. But one thing is certain, William T. Williams, M.T., was no ordinary man—not that any of the mountain men were.

Williams was known to have been a preacher before he went into the Rockies to trap and hunt. He was an educated man, familiar with both Latin and Greek. But it wasn't his language skills that kept him alive in the mountains, where he lived and worked alone, until well past middle age. When he rode, he hunched over the saddle horn, as if asleep, but his keen gray eyes saw everything, and he kept his long rifle ready. Williams bony frame was clothed in leather, shiny from grease and hard wear.

By his own confession Williams could out-drink, out-shoot, and out-trap any other man in the mountains. He claimed to venture farther into hostile Indian territory than his brothers of the buckskin, and said he could swear louder and longer—and in more languages—than anyone alive.

A fixture at the annual Rocky Mountain Rendezvous, Williams eagerly took part in the gambling and drinking, and the shooting matches. Here he put his wits, skills and plain old endurance against the other men who had chosen the lonely existence as their way of life. Old Bill, as he came to be known, frequently was a winner on all counts. But like most of the trappers, he spent the winters at a fort or trading post, not courting danger in the mountains.

Williams happened to be at Bent's Fort on the Arkansas in 1848 when John C. Fremont arrived there on his fourth exploration of the western wilderness. Fremont said to the old Master Trapper:

"Kit Carson was to meet me here and guide me through the San Juans, but I am told he is ill at his home in Taos, and cannot make the trip. I am also told that you are the best man here to find a route through."

"Well, sir," said Williams, "I reckon as how you're right on the last score. I am the best. But I'm not sure whether Kit is sick, or plumb using his head. There's a storm in the mountains the likes of which we haven't seen before. A man would be out of his senses to go up there. Wait till spring and I'll get you through easy."

"A railroad doesn't wait for better weather," Fremont reminded Old Bill. "I need to see the mountains at their worst, to know what to expect."

Williams led Fremont's party of 33 men and 120 pack mules up the Huerfano River, and across the rugged Sange de Cristo Range by way of Robidoux pass. Then they followed the north bank of the Rio Grande through the San Luis Valley. Fremont had written that he expected to follow the Rio Grande to its headwaters in the San Juans, and cross the mountains there. It is probable that the guide knew the pass at the headwaters was impassable in winter, and took the party another route. But from that point their troubles began, and the party was trapped in one of the severest winters known in the San Juans. One-third of the men died, and all of the mules froze to death before they got out of the mountains, thereby establishing Colorado's worst exploring disaster.

In the spring of 1849, Bill Williams and Benjamin Kern were sent from Taos to recover equipment cached on the mountains on the fateful winter trip. Williams and Kern did not return from that journey; instead, they met an ignominious death from Indians, thus ending the career of one of the noted characters of the early days of the mountain states.

THE MAN WHO NAMED DENVER

His voice was weak as the many decades of frontier life exacted their toll. Yet as Charles W. Loving sat on the edge of his bed in Santa Monica, California in 1920, his eyesight and hearing were keen, and his mind clear.

"Yup, I don't care what you've heard about that feller Larimer, or Gov. Denver of Kansas . . . I named the town of Denver, and here's how it happened:

"They was a dozen—maybe 13 of us boys—on our way to the goldfields in Central. 'Twas 1858, 'n I 'member it like it was yesterday. We'd come from I-o-way, an' we'd followed the Platte River most of the way, an we was tired 'n decided to stop 'n rest a few days at the little settlement along Cherry Creek."

The old frontiersman faltered, looked around, then cleared his raspy throat.

"Yup—1858. That's 62 years ago. I was just a pup of 28. But I thought I was an ol' man then! Pshaw! Anyways, we looked around that settlement, an' we figgered it might be a good place for a townsite. It was on the South Platte, 'n on the main route to Salt Lake. 'Sides, that spot, with the Rockies not far away, gave a man the purtiest back yard in the whole country.

"We had an engineer with us, a feller by the name of Parkinson. So we told Parkinson to lay out a townsite, which he did. He made it 220 acres, and one day, while we was all there looking over the plat, an army colonel who was stationed nearby came by with a few of his troops. 'Twas Col. Denver, 'n he says:

" 'What you doin' here, boys?'

"Someone said, 'We're layin' out a town, Colonel.'

" 'Well,' the colonel says, 'What for you layin' out a town here? Ain't no place for a town. It's too far from the mining camps.'

"Somebody says, 'Maybe so, Colonel. But it's on the main route to Salt Lake, 'n it's on the Platte River, 'n the land lies well. 'Sides, it's the purtiest land on the high plains. Takin' everything into 'sideration, it's a real good place for a town.' "

Again Loving paused, toying with his listeners like an angler playing a trout. Then he continued:

" 'So,' the Colonel says. 'Well, maybe so, boys, maybe so. Say, what are you going to call your town, anyway?'

"I spoke right up. 'Why,' I says, 'we're going to name it after you, Colonel.'

"He says, 'You mean you're going to call it Colonel?'

" 'Course not,' I says. 'We're callin' it DENVER. Right, boys?'

"But ol' Colonel Denver throws up his hands, an' he says, 'Oh, don't call it that. Won't never amount to much if you call it that.'

"But I turns to the boys, an' said, 'Let's take a vote on it, right here 'n now. All who's for Denver, stick up a paw.'

"Well, sir, ever last one of 'em voted for Denver. An' the name stuck. We divided up that township, an' each man's share was 42 lots. I gave away seven lots to fellers what wanted to build houses, an' I sold a couple for sacks of flour, 'n a few for gold. But the town didn't grow fast 'nough at first for some of the boys, so they pulled stakes and left their lots to anybody who come along an' claimed 'em."

Charles Loving's voice was barely a hoarse whisper now, and with trembling hands he pulled first his right leg, then the left, onto the bed and settled into the pillows. And, as he closed his eyes, he mumbled:

"Yup, don't know where the rumor started that Larimer laid out Denver. Somebody sure was wrong 'bout that. An' ya' know sumpin' else—the colonel was wrong about that town, too. Denver's still young—may 'mount to sumpin' yet."

PUEBLO DE LECHE

One of the strangest fortifications in early Colorado existed on the banks of the Arkansas River, not far from old Bent's Fort and present day Lamar.

Pueblo de Leche, the Milk Fort, consisted of some thirty small houses, crowded together in an oblong square, with a large center space that was a corral. The houses formed the walls of the fort, with one entrance through a large, stout gate. Built of adobe, some of the houses had an upper story, and most of the rooms inside were whitewashed. In winter they were warm, yet the mud construction provided insulation against the hot sun of summer.

The inhabitants of the Milk Fort were an unusual group of men, women and children; a mixture of French, Spanish, Mexican and Indian. A journalist visiting the fort in 1840 said, "There cannot exist in any nook or corner of the wide universe, a wilder, stranger, more formidable collection of human beings for a civilized eye to look upon. The pencil of old romance would fly from forest cave and daring freebooters, and find here in real life a scene more full of all the best ingredients for all its colors."

Pueblo de Leche took its unusual name from the number of milk goats owned by the residents of the fort. The milk was a comforting sustenance to the people there when buffalo or other game could not be found. And the goats also provided an insurance of sorts to the fort: if besieged by Indians, the people could exist on milk for a far longer time than any marauders would be content to remain in one spot during a raid.

Though considered to be of a peaceful character, the swarthy men of the fort were awesome fighters who could sit their horses as well as any Indian, and shoot accurately with both the bow and a rifle. Most of the men had full beards, and long hair that flowed over their shoulders, which, together with their dark skins and piercing eyes gave them a ferocious appearance. All were armed: some with pistols, but each with a large knife, an ominous weapon if needed.

Pueblo de Leche was a veritable zoo. Dogs, goats, cats, donkeys, tame antelope, buffalo calves and raccoons all were kept by the children, and provided amusement as well as training for future riding skills. Babies were taught to ride horses as soon as they were strong enough to hold on to the animal's mane, often before they could walk.

The fort existed through hunting, trapping, trading with the Indians and the livestock, which were kept in common bands or flocks. Once or twice a year the men would travel to Santa Fe to sell skins and purchase the necessities not available in the wilderness.

An unusual ritual took place at Pueblo de Leche each evening, just before darkness clutched the mud walls in solitude. In great confusion a signal was sounded, and mothers rushed to the center of the fort to get their children out of the corral and into the houses. Then the great door was opened, and in swept the livestock, full of prairie pasture grass, for the evening's confinement.

Though Pueblo de Leche was used only a relatively short time, it provided a colorful wayside in Colorado's ongoing history.

THE FIRST WEDDING

The first wedding ceremony in Larimer County was performed by Bill Sherwood in 1862, under the following circumstances:

Jesse Sherwood, Bill's brother, was justice of the peace. The contracting parties were Lewis Cyr and a daughter of Jesus Louis, of mixed ancestry. They came to the Sherwood ranch, four miles below Fort Collins, to be married. Jesse was away from home, but Bill, who was exceedingly obliging, told them he always tended to his brother's business in Jesse's absence, and he would perform the ceremony.

Jesus Louis, the father of the bride, insisted that there be a marriage contract drawn up before the ceremony took place, and he proceeded to dictate while Sherwood wrote it down:

"You make in the paper, that if my gal behave and boy drink and raise the devil, my gal get all the horses. If my gal do wrong by Lewis he tell her to go hell."

After the paper was prepared, the bride elect, being of a quaint disposition, could not be found when the ceremony was to be performed. She was afterwards discovered under a pile of buffalo robes, and persuaded to complete the contract. During the ceremony the groom discovered he had lost the ring, and became much alarmed. But Bill quieted his fears by telling him that though Jesse always used a ring, he, Bill, had dispensed with it.

Everything then went on without a hitch—except the marriage knot. And though the wedding was of questionable legality, all parties were satisfied, and Jesus Louis had his contract.

THE LEGEND OF SILVERHEELS

Colorado has mountains named for famous politicians, Indians, colleges, and statesmen, but perhaps none was given a title with such affection as Mt. Silverheels, near Fairplay.

Silverheels was a beautiful dancehall girl, one of the most popular in the mining districts. In 1861, she landed in Buckskin Joe, also near Fairplay, where she quickly gained a following of admirers seeking her favors. Buckskin Joe was a typical camp: tents, hotels, brothels, dancehalls, and boarding houses were spotted throughout the area. But at the peak of its activity, the town was hit with the dreaded disease that filled cemeteries and drove others away: smallpox.

Miner after miner came down with the fever, as did camp followers and visitors. And, in the weeks following the onset of the epidemic, only one person showed no regard for her own health as she went from cabin to tent to hotel ministering to the sick and the dying. That person was Silverheels.

Finally, the scourge ran its course, but not before it struck one more victim: the gallant Silverheels. And though she survived the disease, her once-beautiful face was marred with the pock marks that were the aftermath of the illness.

To Silverheels, her face was literally her fortune. Feeling she could no longer confront those who had admired her beauty, she locked herself in her cabin for a solitary recuperation.

As word passed among the miners that Silverheels had been stricken, the men felt concern for her well-being. For not only had they loved her for her beauty, but now they owed her a debt for her self-sacrifice, which they felt they must somehow repay. And, though many were afraid to visit her, most of the men in the camp contributed to a poke of gold dust collected for her, once estimated at being worth in excess of $6,000. A committee was appointed to deliver the gift to Silverheels.

When the delegates knocked on the door of the cabin where the girl lived, there was no answer. Silverheels had no knowledge of their coming, and had left the district without any goodbyes to those who adored and admired her.

A pall settled over Buckskin Joe when it was feared that their kindly nurse would go unrewarded. Rewards were posted and many men searched for her, but she was never found. And, when the thought of finding her finally was given up, and inspired miner looked across the valley and said:

"Let's call that mountain Silverheels, so that we can always remember that sweet little gal."

And though the frontier angel of mercy was never seen again, her memory lives today in the mountain that bears her name.

REMEMBRANCES OF A PROSPECTOR, 1884

". . . Started from Omaha in the spring of 1859. Came across with a mixed train—ox teams and horse teams, five or six wagons connected with our party. Quite a number of others joined us, making 10 to 15 wagons in all. We brought the Rocky Mountain News. Byers was the head of it. He was the proprietor, in connection with a man named Gibbons. There were a great many men coming in just at that time. Some came afoot, some came in handcarts, and one man rolled a wheelbarrow across the plains. We were among the first that came with teams. We did not meet anyone returning until we got within 35 miles from town. All of us came out with the idea that we could get all the gold we wanted, but found it was a humbug at that time . . .

". . . The day before we got through to Denver was the first information we got after the start from Omaha of anything discouraging. Now we had almost to fight our way. There were many discouraging stories. Travel on the Platte mostly turned back a short distance from where we were. Now and again a team went through, but most returned, believing what they heard. And what they heard was the truth, as near as any of them knew it . . .

". . . I worked two or three weeks, then went prospecting to see what could be found. Made the first trip up where Idaho Springs is now. While there, I heard tell of discoveries made at what is now Central and Blackhawk, but there was nobody that knew the way over. The first place was Jackson Diggings, discovered by a man named Jackson where Idaho Springs now stands. Just a few people worked their way in there, following the old road or trail. Some went prospecting in Chicago Creek and Soda Creek, but there was no chance for any number . . .

". . . When I got word of the discovery of Gregory's Diggings, I started there with a party of three or four men. We rigged up a cart with two wheels of a wagon—that was during the month of May, 1859. We got to Gregory's Diggings and stayed there until August. The first discovery was the Gregory Lode. It had free gold near the surface that was sluiced out and washed out fairly well. There was nothing specially of much interest there, except the visit of Horace Greeley. They salted a mine, and deceived him and got a big report of the country from him by that. Still, that mine was a good one, and is a good one until this day . . ."

TRAPPER'S LAKE

It had been a slow day by Trapper's Lake standards. The three fishermen had rowed nearly around the lake, the oarsman trolling Colorado spinners, while the others cast fly after fly to the unwilling trout.

Now, shadows stretched out across the lake as the sun began slipping behind the western range.

The older man knew the lake well. It had long been his favorite dating back to days when he had worked summers in the region. He tried to make at least one trip a year there, preferring the late summer or fall, when fly fishing seemed to be at its best. He spoke of trout in the lake that had his name on them, and he always wanted a contest for the first, the most and the biggest trout. High stakes were bet, sometimes reaching as much as a quarter—though usually a dime.

Many times during the day the old man had pulled out the worn, brown leather fly book from the pocket of his canvas fishing coat. Scrutinizing the patterns closely, he would say:

"Well, this one might just do it. It's been good here before."

And, with the eagerness of a teenager trying to steal a kiss, he would cast again, and again, and again into the choppy waters.

Disgust did not come easily to that older fisherman. He had stood for hours, thigh deep in freezing streams and lakes, casting for reluctant trout, always figuring that one more cast or one more fly would make the difference. But today he had had enough. He was beaten—tired, cold, and angry with the piscatorial god that had defeated him once too often. In a rare, but turgid oath, he said:

"Dammit, let's call it a day."

"Aw, come on Dad. You know this lake better than that. About dark the fish will begin hitting."

"Not for me they won't. I'm going in. You two knuckleheads can stay out here if you want to. I'll go get dinner started. You better get on back to camp in about an hour. It will be dark then."

The wind, which had frothed the lake during the day, was still now as the younger men rowed back to the inlet, across the lake from the trail back to camp. Mountain tops turned from a bluish purple to buffed bronze, in a final salute to the sun. In the after glow the anglers tied on heavily-hackled dry flies, hands shaking from the cold and the fatigue of a day in the boat.

"Let's try it here. We can cast into the inlet and work this whole stretch."

"O.K., but I think we might do better to get out of the boat and fish from shore. They'll be rising in close—if they ever come up at all tonight."

And so they waited for that nirvana of the fly fisherman, the evening rise. Long casts, short casts, different fly patterns—all were tried to no avail. Darkness continued to settle on the lake like an ever-blackening shroud. To change patterns, the anglers had to hold fly and leader overhead, where the lighter sky made it possible to poke the leader through the eye of the hook. But still there had been no action. Finally, one said:

"What do you think? Shall we give it up. Dad will be wondering where we are."

"Yeah, we might as well. I just want to make one or two more casts and I'll be ready to. . . ."

Then it happened. A slap on the water, the automatic tightening of the line, and first one, then the other, had cutthroats battling at the end of the line.

"GOT ONE!" came the shout.

"Me, too!" was the reply.

And for the next few minutes, now in total darkness, the young men experienced one of the fleeting moments of angling that lasts a lifetime. Sometimes the strike came hard, sometimes merely that distinct, quiet "slurp" as a good trout took in a fly.

The reverie was broken by the wave of a flashlight on the distant shore of the lake, and a "ya-hooooo" from an anxious father.

"Come on, we'd better get back. Think I've got my limit anyway."

The trip across the lake was of no consequence to the young men, who were flushed with the excitement of success. When the older man could hear them coming, he began a scolding from the bank that lasted until they had drawn the boat onto the shore. Finally, he said:

"Have any luck . . . you were out there long enough."

"Oh, we got a couple more," said one of the younger men, handing over an open creel that overflowed with fat cutthroat.

"Well, I'll be hornswoggled!"

"UNCLE DICK" WOOTTON

The Pioneer of Pioneers in Colorado
Dying Peacefully at His Home

LIFE OF WONDERFUL ADVENTURE

Sixty years on the Plains and in the Mountains—The Longest Trapping Trip of History, Traversing 5,000 Miles Through the Whole Unvisited Northwest—On Denver's Site Before Others—Owning 160 Acres in the Heart of the Present City—Fighting Indians and Hairbreath Escapes Add Daring Enterprises—A Maker of History and Man of Affairs.

" 'Uncle Dick' Wootton is not expected to live. Hundreds, if not thousands, of the older residents of Denver will be pained to hear of the probable approach of death to this pioneer of pioneers in Colorado. The news received last evening was that Mr. Wootton was lying dangerously ill and very low at his home in Trinidad."

So read the *Denver Republican* November 11, 1891 in a premature obituary that praised the life and the deeds of one of Colorado's best-known trailblazers—the man credited with the development of Raton Pass over the Colorado-New Mexico border.

Richard Lacy Wootton was known as "Uncle Dick" to all, young and old alike. His life story was claimed to be more entertaining than the most famous hero of history. But, given even the exaggeration common in the newspapers of the period, Wootton had to rank high among those whose travels and experiences opened the west for the less adventuresome to follow.

Uncle Dick was born in Virginia, and went with his family to Kentucky at the age of 7. He left home at 17, remaining in the southern states until he was 21, when he joined Governor William Bent's caravan to the Rocky Mountains, which left Independence, Missouri in 1837 with 200 men and 140 wagons of supplies for trading in the fur regions. The party split at Old Bent's Fort on the Arkansas River, near present day La Junta, and Wootton went north with a group that continued trading up to Fort Laramie. There, Wootton left the caravan, and with a new friend—a young man known as Kit Carson—followed a trap line for the next decade.

One tour led Wootton and his party through northwestern Colorado to Utah, up the Green River into Wyoming, along the Big Horn to Montana, then to Idaho and on to Fort Vancouver on the Columbia River. Wootton sold skins at Fort Vancouver, then returned to the starting point on the Arkansas River via California and Arizona. In all, the trip covered nearly 5,000 miles in two years, most of it through virgin territory.

Uncle Dick served as a guide for the army, ran a buffalo farm, drove 14,000 sheep 1,600 miles to California and traded the first barrels of whiskey in the new town of Denver (for which he reportedly was given 160 acres) before he settled in the southernmost part of Colorado. There he established a coal mine, and in 1865, built a toll road over Raton Pass, an endeavor that proved to be rewarding financially in that it provided a direct route from Bent's Fort to Santa Fe on the Old Santa Fe trail.

But Uncle Dick was not without a skeleton in his closet—or at least in his mine shaft. When railroad surveyors were staking a route over Raton Pass in the 1870's, they ran into a solid wall of rock and coal, through which they would have to tunnel at great expense and loss of time. But a man who had worked for Wootton offered to show the surveyors a route, in return for cash. Not trusting the workman, Juan Gallegos, the surveyors wanted proof that he knew the way before paying him the $2,000 he demanded. Gallegos reportedly sent Uncle Dick to assure the surveyors that he knew the way, and Wootton left the camp with a contract to point the way over the Raton range.

Five days after his first visit, Wootton returned to the camp and announced he was ready to lead the stakemen through the pass. When asked about Gallegos, Wootton said he had returned home to Chihuahua, Mexico. The route was staked out over the pass, but Juan Gallegos was never seen again.

Years later, after cataracts had clouded the sight of Uncle Dick, curious explorers found a skeleton at the 200-foot level in Wootton's mine. The skull was crushed, as it might have been in a fall of that distance. Except for a pair of heavy, hob-nailed boots, all clothing and flesh had turned to dust.

When told of the skeleton, Uncle Dick merely wondered whose bones they could be. And, if he knew, he took the secret to his grave on the side of the pass for which he is credited with the discovery.

THE BEGINNINGS OF JULESBURG

In the 1850's Julesburg was the kind of place where a family man travelling through would prefer to leave his wife and children on the stagecoach. A collection of about a dozen buildings was built around the stage station. They included a stable, blacksmith shop, boarding house, warehouse, and the omnipresent saloon, where the bartenders cut the whiskey with water as much as was possible without getting shot.

The town came to be known as the roughest small place between Missouri and the mountains, and oasis for cutthroats and highwaymen who regularly robbed the stagecoaches and mail runs when they weren't gambling for high stakes in the town's gaming rooms.

The founder of Julesburg was a French-Canadian trapper named Jules Beni, who had built a trading post at the "Upper Crossing" of the Platte River on the Overland Stage Route. His post was about a mile east of the mouth of Lodgepole Creek, a favorite crossing and campsite of the Sioux and Cheyenne. When the stage route between Fort Kearney and Denver was laid out in the spring of 1859, Beni was put in charge of the stage station. Jules also was made an agent for the Pony Express division which ran 25 miles northwest of his trading post.

This stage station was at a junction in the line, and housed a telegraph office. It rapidly became one of the most important stops in the Overland Route—and a magnet for the unsavory characters who appreciated the fact that the nearest lawman was 200 miles away.

Among those taking advantage of the absence of authority in the region was Jules Beni himself, who was robbing the stage company on a regular basis. Among other assets he had amassed several thousand dollars worth of stock, which he kept some distance from his station.

In due time, the Overland Stage Company hired James A. "Jack" Slade as a division manager, with the purpose of stopping the disappearance of express along the line. It was not long before Slade fingered Jules Beni as one of those who was robbing the company, and Slade let it be known that either the crimes would stop and Jules pay back what he owed the company, or he would ventilate Jules with a six-shooter.

Now, Jules Beni, by reputation, was not one to back off from a fight. Nor was he the kind to walk into one, if another method would serve his purpose. So, on the next occasion that Slade came into Jules' station, Jules emptied both barrels of a shotgun at him at close range.

A rider was sent for a doctor from Fort Laramie, and Jack Slade, near death, was carried to a boarding house, where he began an almost miraculous recovery from his severe wounds. Determination to get revenge on Jules Beni no doubt played a part in his cheating of death. But Jules had other problems. He narrowly escaped a lynching, and went down the Platte River to wait for the trouble to blow over.

Several months later, Jules Beni returned to the region to get the stock that he had been rounding up over the years. Though Jules was heavily armed and cautious, he was captured by friends of Jack Slade, and taken to a corral in Mud Springs, where he was tied to a center post. Word was sent to Slade of the prize.

It takes little cerebral energy to imagine the meeting between these two enemies when Jack Slade entered that corral. Jules begged for his life—for the sake of his family—offering his stock as a ransom. Slade replied:

"Did you think of my family when you gunned me?"

And with that, Jack Slade began a demonstration of his skill with a pistol, with Jules as the target. Bullet after bullet nipped the hapless Jules Beni, until he was wounded in many places. Slade alternated his marksmanship with drinking and card-playing, as Jules suffered a slow, lingering death, pleading to be killed outright. Finally, when Slade was convinced his shooting ability was appreciated, he executed his enemy. Slade then cut off the ears of Jules Beni. He nailed one to the post of the corral as a warning to others who might commit crimes against the stage company. The other he carried in his pocket: when thrown out on a bar or table, it often was more persuasive than a gun or a knife.

Jules Beni wasn't the only man to meet the punishment of Jack Slade. And, as Slade's reputation grew, the outlaws who had ready access to the riches of the stage lines in his division thinned out. But Slade used little discrimination in dealing with those he assumed guilty, and finally was fired from the company. He later showed up in Montana, where, with some of his old Overland friends, he frequently ended long drinking bouts by shooting up a town. Eventually the Montana Vigilance Committee, then 1000 strong in the Virginia City area, elected to end Slade's terrorism. He died at the end of a rope in March, 1864.

And Julesburg? Its reputation grew rapidly during the early 1860's, as adventurers and newspapermen visited the town to confirm stories—or make up their own about its wickedness. But Indians burned the town to the ground in 1865, thus providing a new start for what now is a crossroads farming community in the northeast corner of Colorado.

"Having sold the Cherry Creek Pioneer press and office to Messrs. Byers and Co. of the Rocky Mountain News, we now bid adieu to our readers and in doing so beg to recommend the News to the public and bespeak for it the patronage which should have been extended to us. We return thanks to Wm. Clancy, Esq., of Nebraska and some few others for their assistance. We are now going to the mountains and instead of picking type we shall try our hand at picking gold."

(Signed)   Jhn. L. Merrick

With that brief notice in an early edition of the *Rocky Mountain News*, John Merrick ended his brief career as a newspaper publisher in Colorado, having assembled the Merrick Press and published one issue of the *Cherry Creek Pioneer*, in 1859 which appeared the same day as the initial issue of the *News*.

But, though Jack Merrick took a respite from newspapering, his press did not, and for the next few years it was used to establish several newspapers in the mining camps. Thomas Gibson, W. M. Byers' partner in the founding of the *Rocky Mountain News*, moved the Merrick Press to Gregory Gulch later in 1859 for the beginnings of the *Rocky Mountain Gold Reporter*, another short-lived venture. Gibson sold the press to Captain West, who founded the *Western Mountaineer* at Golden in December, 1859. The same equipment was used for the publishing of the first issue of the *Canon City Times* in September, 1860, and again for another *Western Mountaineer*, this one published at Laurette, in the Buckskin Joe District of South Park.

But the most intriguing beginnings for a newspaper printed on Jack Merrick's equipment involves community pride and political intrigue of the young towns of Boulder and Valmont in the mid-1860's. The historic Merrick Press had come to rest in Valmont, where a gentleman named Skelton published the first edition of the *Valmont Bulletin*. Valmont, at that time aspired to be the chief city and county seat of Boulder County, and the presence of a newspaper aided in the campaign. Finally, though, a group of citizens could stand the pressure of the *Bulletin* no longer, so they took direct action. On April 1, 1867, they managed to fill Publisher Skelton with the best (or at least strongest) whiskey money could buy, and when Skelton finally felt the need to sleep off a good drunk, they carted the editor, his press and type cases and all other equipment to Boulder.

Well, when Skelton came to, he had become so accustomed to that good Boulder whiskey, that he decided to remain there. And thus the *Boulder Valley News* was launched.

After a series of name changes and mergers with other newspapers, Boulder's initial newspaper was absorbed into the *Boulder Daily Camera*, the newspaper that has served that city since 1891.

And the Merrick Press? After its use in Boulder it was sold to a publisher in Elizabeth, New Mexico, where it very well may have been retired.

HITCH-HIKING

"Aw, come on, Grandpa, What's the matter with hitch-hiking? How else am I going to get a ride? Besides, didn't they do it when you were a kid?"

"Sure they did, Sandy. But it wasn't with a thumb out, taking a chance on a ride with some stranger. Why, I'll bet you thought 'hitch-hiking' is a term you kids invented, didn't you?"

"Well of course, Grandpa. Everyone knows what it means."

"Maybe so . . . maybe they do now. But, let me tell you how it all started:

"Time was when the horse was the main way of getting around this country, and a man with a horse was mobile, could go where he wanted. But, a lot of times when men traveled together, they had only one horse. Now, they both could have ridden, of course, but that would tire the animal, and if they were traveling for any distance, they worked out even a better system."

"What did they do, Grandpa?"

"Well, they would start out together along the road or trail with one man riding and one man walking. Naturally, the man riding would get ahead of the one walking, since the horse moved faster than the man. But, after the rider had gone about a mile, he'd hitch the horse to a tree, and then he'd start walking. Pretty soon, the fellow who had first started hiking would come along to where the horse was, and he'd take the horse, and ride along past the fellow that now was hiking. After that rider had gone about a mile, he'd tie up the horse, and he'd start walking again.

"And that's the way they went, taking turns hitching 'n hiking. And that's how we got the term hitch-hiking. Your Dad and I used to do it when we went up to fish the lakes near Corona Pass."

"Sam, what kind of nonsense are you filling that child with now?"

"Just the truth, Martha, just the truth."

THE MINER'S DELIGHT

The sun chased a warm, bright light over the mountains. Snow-caps glistened and then began to trickle. Spring had arrived, and each creature in its own way was busying itself with a new beginning. As the blanket of winter unfolded, Mother Earth slowly began yielding her vast wealth.

Awaiting the moment when man and beast could survive the high country, miners and settlers gathered at the fringes of the wilderness. All were eager to push forward in search of adventure and riches. The saloons were packed, tension was high, and the air was filled with a strong mixture of smoke, whiskey, and the electrifying excitement of tall tales. The newcomer puffed with expectation, but for the seasoned miner it was only a time to color the disappointments and raise the emotions for another try.

Old timers knew the dangers of life in the hills and maybe this would be their last flirt with life. Would it be the Indians, a grizzly, the elements, or maybe just an empty stomach?

Even today, some parts of the state show the trails, the sluice boxes, and split rocks of those still looking for wealth in the earth. It was there once, could there be more? Ghost towns tell of past glories, but do not encourage a new beginning. And so the old miner, mythical and real, is carried by the winds of time, turning ever so gently in the mind of those who love a dream. For those who do, a warm summer night by the campfire in the gold hills of Colorado might just bring forth a miner's jingle:

> The summers are hot, the winters cold
> An ass, pick, pan, beans, I'm sold
> My hands are tough, like my soul
> A strike, my friends, will make me whole
> A bonanza buys dreams;
>   A few nuggets a bottle and girl. I'm told
> So I sling the pick, swish the pan;
>   Tomorrow I strike the gold.

Gold—the tempting lure. Many tried, some died, and most became its slave.

MINING CAMP JUSTICE

Moving or defacing a claim stake or landmark: "A fine of $50 or three ounces of dust."

Theft above $5, or perjury: "39 lashes on the bare back; confiscation of property and banishment from the District."

Murder: "To be hanged by the neck until dead, dead, dead."

One dead probably would have done the job, but in the Miner's Courts, the jury took no chances. This was an example of justice in the mining districts that sprang to life in Colorado, before more legally-constituted justice followed the prospectors west.

Strict sanitary regulations were observed on some districts, and pollution of a stream used for domestic purposes was subject to a $50 fine.

Questions of guilt or innocence in the Miner's Courts were voted on by ballot, or by arranging different factions of the jury on either side of the room.

Few law books could be found in the camps, but in the population were men of experience and knowledge, who saw the need for establishing laws and officers to enforce them. Yet, the first marshal of Leadville was run out of town after one day in office, the second was murdered, and *his* replacement, an Irishman named Martin Duggan, was threatened hours after he took office.

A brave man, Martin Duggan!

CLANCEY AND THE JUDGE

Billows of muddy water filled Cherry Creek that night in May, 1864. With a crest of 15 feet, the normally small stream slashed through the young community of Denver, carrying away buildings, homes and livestock.

The morning after the storm, crowds of excited townspeople lined the banks of the creek, bemoaning their losses and watching while driftwood, cabins, and the bodies of cattle and sheep went by. Among those suffering loss of a homesite was Judge Apex Bowen, one of early Denver's recognized leaders. Bowen had received the nickname "Apex" after he engineered a wagon road to the top of a nearby grade, and then had designed a strong light to guide travelers. He frequently made reference to the "light on the apex." His given name was forgotten, as was his origin and past history.

Though Bowen was of rough exterior and stern countenance, he was well-educated and persuasive, and somewhat of a leader among the lawless element that had flocked to Denver in those first years. Bowen was elected judge, and his ideas of justice were severe, his methods unique, and he believed strongly in the rights of his office. Woe be to the culprit who offended the dignity of Bowen's court!

But Judge Bowen had suffered more than just the loss of his home and court when the Cherry Creek storm had torn away his cabin. Missing also was Dick Clancey, the Judge's "pard" from early days in the mines, and his long time companion. Bowen had been out with the boys when the crest of the flood hit Denver, and thus had escaped a watery death. But Clancey was no where to be found, and it could only be assumed that he had gone down with the cabin.

Now, Dick Clancey was the opposite of Bowen in many ways, and an unlikely partner and companion for the Judge. Where Bowen was well-read, Clancey was illiterate. While Bowen had a fine command of the language and manners, Clancey was grubby and uncouth, and too fond of distilled spirits. Yet partners they were, and now the Judge loudly lamented the loss of his friend.

The Judge passed the river bank and weepingly declared that Clancey was fit for nothing but the Kingdom of Heaven. Suddenly, he had an idea. Drawing a bottle of rye whiskey from his pocket, he tied a rope around its neck, pushed the cork in firmly, then threw the bottle into the raging torrent as though fishing.

Finally, someone asked Judge Bowen just what he thought he was doing, and Bowen replied:

"Why, don't you know? Last night, while I was out with the boys, my cabin went sailing and Clancey—my ol' pard Clancey—went with it. But if he's in that water, the one thing I know he'll find is a bottle of whiskey, And when he grabs hold of it, I can draw him safely to the land. COME FORTH, CLANCEY, COME FORTH!"

Just then a shout from the crowd caused Judge Bowen to turn around. There was Clancey—his ol' pard Clancey. Pulling the bottle out of the water, Bowen exclaimed:

"Why Clancey, you blamed old cuss! Were you out with the boys, too?"

Susan Underwood 1972

SOAPY SMITH

Con artists and swindlers found easy marks in the mining camps and early cities of Colorado, and surely no huckster cleaned out pockets any better than Jefferson Randolph Smith—better known as Soapy Smith.

Soapy earned that sobriquet in Leadville and Denver, where he sold bars of soap with $5, $10; and even $100 bills wrapped around them. Oddly, the only ones who ever managed to buy those lucky bars were confederates of Soapy's.

His greatest con was at Creede, where for several months he displayed what he claimed was a petrified man of early Asian descent—a great archeological find.

But, even a con man like Soapy was not all bad. His cousin, Colonel Edward B. Smith, of Washington, D.C., once said of Soapy:

"I knew Jefferson from the time he was born. No man of my acquaintance had a fairer start or commanded a better prospect for life than did the same Jeff Smith of whom the world heard so much that was not complimentary while he lived and when he died. His family was equal in standing to any in Georgia, both his father and mother descending from long lines of well-known people. His mother was a lovely, Christian woman, his father a college-bred man and lawyer of good standing.

"Jeff was the oldest of four children, and when it became necessary to go to work on the family farm, he proved a veritable prodigy. He was full of push, delighted in outdoor life, and withall was shrewd and energetic, a good manager as well as hard worker. By the time he was 10 years old he was doing a man's work and was directing things in a way that would have done credit to one of mature years."

Now, to say that Colonel Smith's view of his cousin was slightly prejudiced might be begging the point, but in relating the life of Jefferson Randolph he did leave out a few important details, such as the petrified man, and Soapy's sleight of hand tricks with the bars of soap. But Colonel Smith did relate the fact that though Soapy was hard working as a youngster, he became enamored with the life of the drummer, for he was a fluent talker and deft salesman of everything from pocket combs to elixirs. And if Soapy stretched the truth now and then or made a switch of merchandise during a sale—well, that was just his style. One time in Colorado City, Soapy had gathered a crowd around his stand, and was saying:

"Gentlemen, I am not here to indulge in wild flights of oratory but to tell you a plain story. Twenty years ago, I came up from Texas on a trapping expedition. While alone in the wilds of Routt County, I met an Indian. He seemed a man of principle, and in a day or two he quite won my confidence. But alas!"

"What happened, Soapy," someone shouted.

"He was playing possum on me. His object was to lull my natural distrust, for there I was, a hundred miles from the nearest white man, and unsuspicious as a year-old babe.

"Well, sir, one night after the Indian and I had had a long talk on religious matters, I lay down to sleep with no more fear than you will have in your homes tonight. About midnight, I awoke to find the Indian had me by the hair. 'What do you want,' says I. 'Your scalp,' says he. 'But I can't spare it,' says I. 'You'll have to,' says he. And, thereupon he ran a knife around a portion of my scalp and yanked off my top knot."

"And then you shot him, didn't you, Soapy?" a man asked.

"No, my friends. Other men in my place would have done so, but I couldn't bring myself to do it. I simply told him that any man who would do so mean a trick would never prosper. Then I packed up my traps and left the place. But, right here and now I will place my hand on the place where I was scalped . . . there."

"Aw, come on, Soapy. You've got hair there," said a skeptic.

"So I do, gentlemen, so I do. None of you would ever know I had been scalped, had I not told you. But, when I returned to civilization, it was my good fortune to meet Professor Grimshaw, the celebrated chemist and pharmacist. After we had shaken hands, he says, 'What are you doing running around with a scalped head?' Well, naturally, I says, 'I can't help it.' He says, 'Of course you can.' And right then and there, he handed me the formula for a hair restorer that you can buy right here today for a mere 25¢ a bottle. It prevents hair from falling out, and will grow hair where there is none. Why, I caution folks to wear gloves if they use it often, or they may end up with hair on their palms. Now, even if you get scalped half a dozen times, there's enough in this 25¢ bottle to grow luxurious tresses once again. Try it, my friends, and accept no other."

That was Jefferson Randolph Smith, king of the high country con men. Soapy left Colorado to answer the call of the Klondike, and was killed in a gunfight in Skagway, when for once, someone else's hand was faster than his.

END OF AN ERA

"What do I hear for this plow? The wood is still sturdy, and the point shows only a little minor wear. Will someone give me $5 . . . do I hear $5 . . . I have $4, thank you, sir . . . now do I hear $5"?

And so the auction began with the clamor for bids and ended with the gavel rapping down the final sale. For the buyers it was a time to see friends, exchange gossip, and hopefully make some useful and money-saving purchases.

Little if any thought was given to the aged couple waiting in the parlor. The history of their lives was spread over the front and back yard. Yet, in but one day a large share of their life's accumulation would be bundled up, tied down, and then carried away.

As the sun pushed morning aside and brought in afternoon, picnic lunches were spread out by those waiting for some of more choice items being saved for the last. The meal was casual but filling—fried chicken, deviled eggs, potato salad, fresh baked bread and a dipper of cool well water to clear the throat. But, inside, the owners, "Ma" and "Pa" as their grown children so fondly called them, experienced the anxiety of parting with something so dear. Remembrances of past days came swiftly now—the rope swing gently playing in the breeze, where but a short time ago a squealing little girl delighted at a father's playful push; a set of child's gardening tools, the tall leafy maple tree in the front, planted by their son when he was three.

"What do I hear for this fine milking cow . . . here's a good Boston rocker, just well broke in . . . now, where can you find sad irons like these . . . who needs a set of china . . ."

On it went, until the shadows of evening began feeling their way across the land. And, when the auctioneer gaveled away their last treasure, the old couple stood in the dimness of their room, holding hands, eyes blurred, neither daring to speak.

JAMES P. BECKWOURTH — GOOD MEDICINE

Whether he was called Jim Beckwith as christened, or James Beckwourth, as he later preferred, this adopted chief of the Crow Indians was one of the true characters of the American west.

James Beckwourth was born in Virginia from the relationship of a Negro slave and an Irish overseer. His father acknowledged young Jim, and tried to direct him into the trade of blacksmithing, after they had moved to St. Louis in the early 1800's. But the young man and the smithy found themselves at odds, and Jim decided he didn't want to argue with a man who could use a hammer as well as the blacksmith could.

Jim left home at the age of 19, encouraged partly by an enraged father whose daughter consumed the young man's passion. That the girl had succumbed to his entreatments was not surprising; from his earliest days, Jim had charisma. He was strong, handsome, willful and charming, and had a mind that was quick and challenging.

But, if anyone understood young Jim's plight when confronted by a pregnant girl, it was Jim's father. So when Jim decided it was time for him to begin traveling, his father provided $500 and a good horse, and Jim took the trail that eventually led him into the mountains of Colorado.

Somewhere between his youth and his appearance in the mountains, Jim Beckwith became James P. Beckwourth. But the basic nature of the man did not change: courageous, enterprising, one who respected the talents of others, and who quickly could adapt to his surroundings. Though he professed to only four years of schooling in St. Louis, Jim was well-read and a superb conversationalist. But, most of all, he was a storyteller, with an unsuppressed ego.

Just about everything that happened to *any* frontiersman happened to Jim Beckwith, to hear him tell it. Attacks by wild animals, long periods of denial of food and other supplication, harassment by hostile Indians, all were part of the repertoire of his inventive mind and supple tongue. Most of his acquaintances found it difficult to know where Jim's experiences stopped and his imagination took over—if indeed they cared.

Yet James P. Beckwourth did have enough adventures of his own to make his life story read like the wildest fiction. He worked as a hunter with the army, and as a guide for the ill-fated William Henry Ashley expedition into northern Colorado in the winter of 1823-24. Ashley was not prepared for the blizzards and depredation that met this trip, though the expedition was considered a success and Beckwourth was well-rewarded for his services.

In the middle 1820's Beckwourth's affinity for the Indians became apparent, to the point that a fellow mountain man, Caleb Greenwood, reportedly told a band of Crow Indians that Jim was the son of a Crow chief, stolen as a youngster by Cheyennes, and later raised by white men. Greenwood told the story in fun, but later, when Beckwourth was running a trap line with Jim Bridger, Beckwourth was captured by a Crow war party, and the story saved his life. In fact, the wife of a dead chief identified him as her son by a mole on his eyelid. Beckwourth took an Indian bride, and lived, worked and fought with the Crows for several years, rising to the position of chief of the tribe.

Sometime after he left the Crows, Jim lived in California, then returned to St. Louis for a short visit. He came west again in 1859, this time to Denver, with the A. P. Vasquez and Company train of merchandise. His return to Colorado stirred the redman brothers, who considered him to be the "Big Medicine" of all the white men on the plains. During the period Jim lived in and near Denver, it was not uncommon to find up to twenty Cheyenne or Arapahoe teepees at his place.

Beckwourth had an interest in the Civil War, and tried to get a commission in the Second Colorado Regiment. Failing that, he did serve again as an army scout, and was one of the guides that led Colonel Chivington and his troops to the camp of the Cheyennes and Arapahoes in November, 1864, at the time of the infamous Sand Creek Massacre—an act that Beckwourth regretted the rest of his life.

All this time, Jim Beckwourth had not been forgotten by his Crow tribesmen. Envoys were sent to entreat him to return at least for a visit to their camp at the headwaters of the Missouri. Finally, he consented, and once at the camp, he was treated with all the respect of the great chief he had been. Jim stayed several weeks with the Crows, during which they used every argument and enticement they could to get him to remain with them as their chief. But Beckwourth refused. Finally, upon his preparations to return to Denver, a feast of roast dog was prepared in his honor. When Jim ate the meat that had been served him, he died on the spot, having been poisoned by the Indians. W. N. Byers, editor of the *Rocky Mountain News* and a former neighbor of Jim's in Denver, reported:

"The Crows freely acknowledged the crime, saying: 'He has been our good medicine. We have been more successful under him than under any chief.' Their excuse was that if they could not have him living, it would be good medicine to have him dead."

Thus, James P. Beckwourth remained with his adopted people, writing the final chapter in the life of one of that rare breed—the mountain men.

A Portrait of Colorado

Art and Photography Identification:

Front of dust jacket: Abandoned mill, Empire
P. 5, Covered wagon, Estes Park
Pp. 6-7, Mule deer
Pp. 8-9, Snowfield, Steamboat Springs
P. 11, Ore car
P. 13, East of Pagosa Springs
P. 14, Magpie
P. 15, Wittemeyer's Wagon, Sunshine Canyon, near Boulder
P. 16, Lantern, near Rifle
P. 17, Corn crib, near Sterling
P. 19, Sleigh, between Magnolia and Pinecliffe
P. 20, Fence post
P. 21, Highway 160, East of Alamosa
P. 23, Colorado and Southern caboose, Silver Plume
P. 25, Weeds, near Limon
P. 26, Rain barrel, Silver Plume
P. 27, Miners Exchange, St. Elmo
Pp. 28-29, South of Steamboat Springs
P. 31, Blacksmith shop, Hygiene
P. 32, Pully, Redcliff
P. 33, Yucca, near Pueblo
P. 35, Two dogs, Alma
P. 37, Pruitt Horse Ranch, Turkey Creek Canyon
P. 39, Roadside minutia
Pp. 40-41, Barn, Valmont Road, Boulder
P. 42, Barn, Mancos
P. 43, Ouray
P. 45, Turkey Vulture
P. 47, Colorado & contrasts
P. 49, Hiram Fuller House, Boulder
P. 50, Rissen Church, Boulder
P. 51, Adobe house, Ft. Garland
P. 52, Roundhouse, Como
P. 53, Water wagon, Alma
P. 55, Garden of the Gods
P. 56, Sunset Mill, between Boulder and Ward
P. 57, Porch, Georgetown
P. 59, Pikes Peak
Pp. 60-61, School and church, Westcliffe
P. 63, Treasure Falls, Wolf Creek Pass
P. 65, Roof, Georgetown
P. 66, Cattle loader, near Rifle
P. 67, Landscape between Julesburg and Holyoke
Pp. 68-69, Foothills ranch, near Lyons
P. 70, Hardware store, Silverton
P. 71, Back Range from Peak-to-Peak Highway
P. 72, Adit, Silver Plume
P. 73, Button shoe, Sunshine Canyon
P. 75, Blue Mesa, west of Gunnison
P. 77, Ivie Barn, New Castle
P. 79, Sunset, near Wray
P. 80, South Park City Post Office
P. 81, Derelict, Silver Cliff
P. 82, Silver Plume
P. 83, Longs Peak
P. 84, Maxwell House, Georgetown
P. 85, Window and chair, Florence
P. 86, Chair, Rollinsville
P. 87, Berthoud Pass
P. 88, Georgetown school
P. 89, St. Marys Lake derelict
P. 91, Red rocks near Morrison
P. 92, Homestead, near Rifle
P. 93, Milk can, Silver State Dairy
P. 95, Cabin between Nederland and Ward
P. 96, Bell tower, Ward
Back of dust jacket: Sunrise, Estes Park